The
Commitment
Dialogues

The
Commitment
Dialogues

How to Talk Your Way Through the Tough Times and Build a Stronger Relationship

Matthew McKay, Ph.D., and Barbara Quick

McGraw·Hill

New York   Chicago   San Francisco   Lisbon   London   Madrid   Mexico City
Milan   New Delhi   San Juan   Seoul   Singapore   Sydney   Toronto

The **McGraw·Hill** Companies

Library of Congress Cataloging-in-Publication Data

McKay, Matthew.
    The commitment dialogues : how to talk your way through the tough times and
build a stronger relationship / by Matthew McKay, and Barbara Quick. — 1st ed.
        p.   cm.
    ISBN 0-07-144155-7
    1. Man-woman relationships.   2. Interpersonal relations.   3. Commitment
(Psychology).   I. Quick, Barbara.   II. Title.

    HQ801.M487725   2005
    306.7—dc22   2004015656

1 2 3 4 5 6 7 8 9 0   FGR/FGR   0 9 8 7 6 5

ISBN 0-07-144155-7

McGraw-Hill books are available at special quantity discounts to use as premiums and
sales promotions, or for use in corporate training programs. For more information, please
write to the Director of Special Sales, Professional Publishing, McGraw-Hill, Two Penn
Plaza, New York, NY 10121-2298. Or contact your local bookstore.

This book is printed on acid-free paper.

In memory of my mother, Louise,
whose commitments were unswerving.
—MM

For my son, Julian, who taught me the true meaning
of long-term commitment.
—BQ

Contents

Introduction

———————◆———————

Everyone harbors a desire, no matter how deeply buried, to love and be loved in a relationship that will withstand the test of time.

So why do so many of us, fueled by this desire, try and fail? Why—even in the presence of a potential partner who seems to have all the right stuff—do so many people have trouble crossing the chasm between dating and long-term commitment? Why is it that so many, attempting that leap, find themselves confronted with problems and emotions that were completely under wraps during the courtship phase of their relationship?

These are some of the questions we've set out to answer in this book. Whatever wisdom is contained in these pages should be credited to Dr. McKay's clients who, over the past twenty-five years, had the courage to journey into the depths of their relationship pain.

It is from these clients that the authors have learned to recognize the four primary fears that tend to undermine long-term love: the fear of engulfment, the fear of abandonment, the fear of shame, and the fear of emptiness.

The first four chapters of this book are devoted to explicating these fears. By eavesdropping on other couples' therapy—meeting the individuals involved, hearing their stories, witnessing their struggles, and sitting in the therapist's chair, as it were, while they journey toward insight—you'll learn to recognize how each of these four fears works to sabotage commitment. At the end of all but one chapter—in this first part and throughout the rest of the book—there are exercises designed to help you and your partner recognize the presence of these fears in your relationship, so that you can get beyond them.

There is no formula that will make commitment foolproof or easy. But uncovering those fears that you or your partner have brought into your relationship from the past can go a long way toward clarifying your hopes, desires, and needs in the present and for the future.

Any successful relationship between two people necessitates a process of give-and-take, learning and acceptance, insight, compassion, and goodwill. It is not just a matter of finding the right mate and then staying frozen in some happy moment in time. People change and grow within love relationships. The relationships themselves may have to radically change to survive the changing circumstances of life: children, illness, financial problems, career upheavals . . . The list goes on and on.

But there are common themes that emerge in most all couple's therapy. The presenting problems—conflicts over money, sex, children, time, control, where to live, how to live—are almost always symptomatic of deeper fears for which one's partner may simply be the trigger.

Chapters 5 through 10 will show you—again, through other couples' stories and struggles—how to look beneath the surface of "presenting problems" to the fears that underlie them. Each chapter tells the story of one couple, lets you listen in on their therapy dialogue, and takes you on the same journey we took in learning to understand what it meant. Each of these chapters also ends with exercises and assessments that will promote insight into your own or your partner's fears, with guidelines for overcoming them.

These deep fears, with their roots in childhood, send out tendrils that can strangle even the most promising romantic bond. It's never enough to snip away at the tendrils; the underlying fears themselves must be rooted out and exposed. The couple as a unit must commit themselves to dealing with these fears when they emerge. Fears that continue to exert their powerful, hidden influence unabated are likely to sabotage your relationship.

If you are romantically drawn to individuals who shun commitment, you yourself may be influenced by one of the four fears explored in this book. Your own fears can remain safely unacknowledged so long as your partner is the one who seems to be doing the running. It's important to honestly examine your own patterns. A history of involvements with commitment-phobic people suggests that you have work to do on your own hidden fears.

Let's get started.

Author's Note

The examples of commitment struggles and triumphs you'll witness are based on couples I've worked with in my professional practice. Identifying details have been changed; weeks of therapy have sometimes been telescoped into one or two sessions. But in every case my coauthor and I have been faithful to the emotional truth of each couple's story.

—MATTHEW McKAY

PART I

---◆---

The Core Fears
Buried Inside Relationships

You're about to meet four couples, one in each of the four chapters that follow. You'll "see" these men and women as I first saw them when they walked into my consulting room, telling me as much with their body language and gestures as they did with the words they chose to describe why they'd come in for couple's therapy. You will be a fly on the wall in one of the most private of places, where people bare their hearts to a caring stranger in the hope that he or she may be able to help them find happiness. You will bear witness to a most frightening process, in which two people who love each other finally let down their guard and bare their hearts.

Each of these couples will show you through the story of their therapy how to recognize and uncover one of the four fears that undermine long-term relationships. Jared and Laney will be your guides through the fear of engulfment. Gary and Sierra will shine a light in the darkest reaches of the fear of abandonment. Todd and Jacklyn tear the wrapping off the fear of shame. And Guy and Danielle will give you a long hard look into the fear of emptiness.

You may recognize yourself in some of these stories. Or you may recognize the person you love—and even people you've loved at other times in your life. Recognition of these fears in yourself and others is the first step toward getting beyond them.

The Fear of Engulfment

Will I Still Exist if I Merge with You?

Jared and Laney are both formidable individuals—it's obvious from the moment they walk into my consulting room.

Jared, a man somewhere in his early forties, has the face of an emperor on a Roman coin. His striking features, along with his stocky build and plummy British accent, make his presence a little intimidating.

In her initial conversation with me on the phone, Laney described Jared as "a card-carrying grown-up." A scientist in a highly visible field, he enjoys a world-class reputation and travels between the United States and Europe several times a year.

Jared is clearly uncomfortable finding himself in my office. But he meets my eyes when we shake hands, and I catch a humorous glint there—a sort of tip-off that this was all Laney's idea and he's only there to please her.

Laney sounded like a very no-nonsense sort of person on the phone. She described herself as a thirty-five-year-old divorcée, a writer, and a teacher. She has one of the much-sought-after faculty positions in the English department of our local state college, which is well known for its excellent writing program. A published poet who has picked up a couple of awards along the way, Laney told me that she's halfway through her first novel.

Having set up my expectations based on her phone introduction, I am surprised by Laney's physical presence, which is much more exotic than I had expected from hearing her voice. She walks into the room with the graceful resignation of a woman who is used to men finding her beautiful. As different as these two seem from one another, they possess an identical sadness about them. But, of course, most people coming into my office look either anxious, sad, or angry.

Unlike Jared, Laney also looks vulnerable—openly, honestly, transparently so. I can see her taking in everything—me, my office, Jared's body language as he sits down on the one straight-backed chair in the room. It is also clear to me that she feels, as well as notices, everything around her.

After three years of dating Jared, Laney is ready to progress to the next level of commitment in their relationship. She says she's tired of being each other's houseguest: she wants to move in together. Jared is convinced that living together would be a disaster. Laney, who told me that she's aware of some of Jared's underlying issues, has turned to couple's therapy in hopes of seeing their issues resolved.

Jared and Laney have been seeing each other four nights a week. It's a part-time and yet an exclusive relationship for both of them: they each have other close friends, but neither of them dates anyone else.

Jared likes things just as they are. He doesn't seem at all unsure about Laney, or to be holding out for someone "better." In fact, I am impressed by how very easily he expresses his love and admiration for her. But he seems much more interested in an ongoing romance than in forming a committed partnership. Like Laney, he's already been married. It's married life, Jared says, not Laney, that presents the problem for him.

Laney says that she likes the idea of marriage; she always has. She just thinks she married the wrong man the first time. Once their initial infatuation wore off, she and her ex found that they weren't compatible on a day-to-day basis. Each ended up trying, in vain, to change the other.

She and Jared, by contrast, get along beautifully—apart from their opposing views on the idea of moving in together and merging their lives. On long trips together, she's been amazed at how compatible they are and how easy it is to spend time in each other's company.

And their relationship has maintained a passionate intensity that both of them value.

But Laney has noticed Jared's pattern of pulling away—into work obligations or solitary travel—after times of particular closeness between them. She says that no matter how clearly she sees the pattern and has even come to expect Jared's periodic retreats from closeness, his behavior still hurts her every time. She has reached the point where she's ready to give up on Jared if he remains unmovable. She wants more than he's offering her now: she wants a partner in life.

Laney and Jared's Commitment Dialogue

Laney: What I'm asking for is completely normal. I mean, it's normal to want to be together and make a life together if you love someone. Isn't it?

Jared: Laney and I have spoken of this a thousand times. Living together doesn't work for me. I know what would happen—I'd get all emotionally withdrawn. Family life doesn't work for me.

Jared's blanket statement that family life doesn't work for him is a tip-off that he's responding from a set of beliefs that predate his relationship with Laney by many years. He's told me without saying so directly that there's something about family life that's extremely frightening to him—maybe even in a way that feels life threatening. The difficult thing is to get Jared to go to this place without shutting down.

Dr. McKay: Jared, I'd like you to think a little bit about what your life would be like if you and Laney lived together. Think about a typical day. You and Laney wake up in the same bed together. And maybe you have tea in bed and read the paper. Then you shower and get dressed. You each go off to work, and then in the evening you come home and Laney's there. Maybe she's made dinner for you. Or you both decide to go out for dinner or a drink, maybe meet some friends. Then you come home and maybe you make love and go to sleep in the same bed. What is it about that scenario that feels scary to you?

Jared: Well, what you've described is very much the way things are with us now on the four nights a week we spend together. And it's not scary at all. It's extremely pleasant. But it would be different if we merged our lives and moved in. There would suddenly be all these things I'd be expected to do—all the things Laney gets done herself when I'm not there, and that I get done on my own at my house. Repairs and things. And all the everyday chores that have to do with running a household—it's all very antiromance. Things like putting out the recycling and making sure there's enough toilet paper. And then there's the issue of someone expecting you to show up at a certain time and being really hurt and disappointed in you if you don't. And maybe getting angry at you, too.

Dr. McKay: Have there been times in the past when Laney has gotten angry at you for not meeting her expectations?

Jared: Not per se. But I'm sure that would be the case, eventually, if we were to move in together.

Dr. McKay: It sounds as if there's something about the idea of living together that feels wrong to you, Jared. Dangerous. That would put you in a position that might feel very painful.

Jared: When you live with someone, your range of choices is radically diminished. Your life is dictated by the other person's needs and expectations of you. You have to go along with what they want.

Dr. McKay: Or what?

Jared: Or you're in for a lot of unpleasantness.

Dr. McKay: So unless you do everything Laney wants and expects from you in a living-together situation, she's going to withdraw her love?

Jared: Yes—that's about it. I'll feel like no matter what I do, it'll never be enough. She'll never be happy with me.

Dr. McKay: What are some of the things you think Laney would be unhappy about?

Jared: I don't know. She'd expect me to be there at a particular time every night.

Laney: I wouldn't! You know, we usually meet pretty late for dinner, anyway. I like to go to the gym in the early evening or take a walk or sit at a café and write. I don't have any particular agenda about what time you'd have to come home.

Jared: Well, okay. But there'd be all these things you'd want me to do around the house and in the yard. I'd suddenly have all these things I'd have to get done so I couldn't just do whatever I wanted to. I wouldn't be able to relax. Weekends would just become a string of chores and family obligations—I've seen it happen. And you'd hate me hanging about with my friends instead of spending all my time with you. You'd start telling me I drink too much, and you'd want me to exercise more and pretty soon I wouldn't even recognize my own life. That's how it works when people move in together—they spend all their time doing chores and running errands. And if you don't manage to do what the other person wants you to—if you fall short of their expectations—you're made to feel worthless, like you'll never be good enough.

Dr. McKay: So you think Laney is going to turn into a really demanding person who will make you tow the line. And if you don't, you're going to have to feel really awful about yourself.

Jared's expectations of what might happen in a more committed relationship with Laney seem to have been formed from experiences he had long before he even met her. It's time to start linking up Jared's fears about moving in with Laney with lessons he carries with him from his past.

Dr. McKay: Does the prospect of living together and feeling like you'll never be able to do enough, no matter how hard you try, remind you of anything?

Jared: Well, I'm not an idiot. My mother was a super-controlling person, and nothing I did was ever good enough as far as she was concerned. But she also micromanaged every aspect of my life, at least as far as she was able to. When I was sent away to boarding school at the age of eleven, it was a relief, let me tell you! I dreaded going home at the holidays. School wasn't always very nice, but it was more like home than home ever was. My mother disapproved of every friend I ever made, every girl I ever liked—no one was good enough for me, even though I was never good enough for anything.

Dr. McKay: That sounds like a total nightmare, Jared. I can understand how you would have made the decision long ago to never, ever again let yourself feel so vulnerable to another person's expectations—never again to be in a position where someone else has the power to make you feel so much pain. But, tell me. You're a man of science. What evidence do you have that Laney would be like your mother? What have you experienced with her that makes you think that she would behave in similar ways?

Jared: Quite honestly, I can't say that I have absolute evidence. But based on my own personal experience, I know that things would get very bad very fast.

Dr. McKay: Let me ask you something. Let's imagine you and Laney living together. Let's imagine that there are times when you disagree about something. You want to go out for dinner, but Laney wants to cook dinner at home. Or you want to go skiing over the holidays, but she wants to visit her family. You want to read the paper, but she wants to talk with you about her writing. You want to spend some time visiting a friend, but she wants you to do something with her. What do you think will happen? How do you think the two of you would navigate those conflicts if you were living together?

Jared: I just feel that it wouldn't work for me. I would be so intensely uncomfortable.

Dr. McKay: What do you think would happen, though, between the two of you? You'd be uncomfortable—that's number one. What else?

Jared: I think she'd be very upset.

Dr. McKay: So you'd be uncomfortable, and she'd be upset. How would she be upset—in what way?

Jared: I have to say, what Laney wants isn't unreasonable. I really don't see it that way. I just see myself as sort of unreasonable.

Dr. McKay: But she'd be upset. What kind of upset would that be, and how would she express it?

Jared: It wouldn't be so much what she would say. It would be what she wouldn't say. It would be the way she would look at me, withering kinds of looks.

Dr. McKay: You'd get withering looks. And would she be cold and distant emotionally?

Jared: I think I'm the one who would be cold. I know I would simply withdraw emotionally. I would not be there.

Dr. McKay: But what would she do? She'd be withering in her demeanor.

Jared: She would make me feel so guilty.

Dr. McKay: What would she say to you that would make you feel guilty? How would she treat you?

Jared: I suppose she would express, as she does so well, the rightness of her position, the normalcy of her position.

Dr. McKay: So what it feels like is that if you're living together, and you have conflicts, she's going to be righteous. She's going to be angry and withering if you don't go along with what she wants.

Jared: Or hurt and withering.

Dr. McKay: And you're going to feel guilty and really bad about yourself—

Jared: Yes!

Dr. McKay: —and your withdrawal. I'm going to ask you another question. Are there any conflicts that you have now about things where you want it one way, she wants it another, and you may not express how you feel? I'm wondering if there are any conflicts where you're aware that you really are kind of pulling in different directions.

Jared: I can think of various times when she's asked me quite nicely, has been quite reasonable, if I might do something with her and her mother. And, you know, I've done it. But frankly, it's not my idea of a fun thing to do on the weekends. I already went through all that with my own aged parents, and now I'm done. I just find it an imposition, the idea that I have to go through it all over again. Laney had asked me if at least once a month I could do something with her and her mother, and, you know, I don't want to be a complete ogre about it. And so I did it.

Laney: You did it *once* this past year.

Dr. McKay: Let's stay with this, Jared. What do you think would happen if you said to Laney, "You know what? I really don't want to step in and be part of someone else's family. I don't really want to go and hang out with you and your mother. It's not my preference. It's not something I'm comfortable with." What do you think would happen between you?

Jared: Well, you know, for me it's really been walking a fine line, because at a certain point, I know, she'll just throw up her hands and say, "You're not involved enough. This isn't enough for me." So I want to give enough to keep her in my life, because I love her dearly and enjoy her company enormously. But if I give over too much, it won't work for me anymore, because I'm not a family sort of guy.

Dr. McKay: So she'd throw up her hands. Does that mean she'd give up the relationship?

Jared: She'd walk away if I gave *too* little. If I didn't measure up to what she considers an acceptable level of involvement.

Dr. McKay: Would it start with the withering looks and that righteous sense that you weren't living life the way you should, you weren't giving as much as you ought to?

Jared: Yes, I think that's right.

Dr. McKay: What would you like to say to her about her mother and the role she plays in your relationship?

Jared: I've already gone through this with my own parents. I saw it through to the end, and I did what I was supposed to do. But I'm done with it now. I don't want to go through it all over again. I guess I'd like to say, "Look, my dear, I'm not the right one to do this. I'm not good at family life. I don't know how to do it, and it makes me uncomfortable."

Dr. McKay: And if you said that, you're afraid that she'd throw up her hands or get withering.

Jared: I guess I feel that she'd walk, because I wouldn't be meeting her expectations about what she thinks a partner should do.

Dr. McKay: Laney, what's happening to you as you listen to Jared right now? What's your reaction? He's afraid you're going to walk and be really, really righteous and upset. What *is* happening to you?

Laney: It hurts me, in a way. I feel sad, because I'd love it if he could open his heart more to my family. I actually think he could find some healing there, if he just gave them and himself half a chance. But all along I've known that Jared is Jared. I know what he's like. And this relationship is full of compromises for me. I'm used to compromising, in terms of what I want—because, obviously, the payoffs are great enough to justify the compromise. What we share together— just the two of us—is really special.

Dr. McKay: Jared's saying that he's expecting that you'll be kind of angry, withdrawn, withering, and then, eventually, throw up your hands and leave. Is that what you are feeling as you listen to him?

Laney: I think it's silly. I've never really gotten very upset . . . I think there was one time I got really angry with Jared, at a party, when I felt he treated me badly, and I really was upset, and I did walk out. I left.

Dr. McKay: But regarding this issue, is he reading you right? Or has he gotten you confused with someone else or something else?

Laney: It's not me. I don't really get angry. That's not my style.

Dr. McKay: And you wouldn't throw away the relationship because he didn't want to spend a day with you and your mother?

Laney: No—not because of that. My brothers both live close enough to help—it's not like I feel completely alone with her. It's just the idea that Jared won't even think about living together that exasperates me, that makes me think about giving up on him. But, you know, I'm not very good at leaving him.

Dr. McKay: Now, Jared, this is interesting. Laney's really saying that no, she isn't about to quit the relationship if you're not prepared to spend time with her family. I'm wondering what you think about the difference between your prediction that she's going to be disgusted and withering and eventually leave and what we're hearing from Laney right now.

Jared: I don't know what to say, really. I guess when we *have* put it to the test, it's true—that's not how she's acted in the past.

At this point, we have a critical moment in our therapy dialogue, because we're finding out that Jared's picture of reality is different from what really exists in the relationship between him and Laney. His picture of reality is very much based on his experience with his mother. He expects to be rejected. He expects withering looks. He expects to lose Laney if he lets her know his limits. What I have to do now is to draw Jared into a social experiment, to find out whether that picture of reality derived from his life with his mother is real with Laney, or whether it's something left over from an old time, an old life.

Dr. McKay: So right now, Jared, I guess I'm asking you to consider this as an experiment. You're a scientist. Right now we're experimenting to find out whether the hypothesis that Laney might respond like your mother is true or perhaps not-so-true. And the first little bit of evidence we've gathered is that Laney's saying she basically already knows that you're not going to be very involved with her family and so has not assumed that that was going to be part of the relationship. In fact, usually efforts to get you to join her and her mother don't work out that well, and she's learned to live with that. How does that fit with your idea of the way things are?

Jared: I suppose it's accurate; it's an accurate assessment. Laney keeps her grievances pretty much to herself.

Dr. McKay: So you're not sure if she's really being completely honest with you.

Jared: It's not that; Laney is quite open about her feelings. But she's not a whiner.

Dr. McKay: What else do you think you'd need to say "no" to, if you were living with Laney? What else would you need to let her know you couldn't do?

Jared: In the past when I lived with someone, a lot of what I liked or felt comfortable with when we were dating changed once we moved in together. I lived with a woman who is now a very dear friend of mine. When we started out, she had all these women friends. She'd have her women's nights out, and she'd do a lot of things with them. And then I'd have a lot of free time. I'd have my nights out with my friends or by myself. But, all of a sudden, you know, when we started living together, she wanted to spend every night together. She wanted to sit on the sofa and watch videos. She stopped being the fun, busy person she'd been. It just got to be an incredible drag!

Dr. McKay: What do you think would happen if you lived with Laney? The same thing? She'd suddenly want to spend all that time with you, time you'd rather have for your own pursuits?

Jared: I'm quite sure of it. Everything changes when two people merge their lives. There'd be nothing left of me. There would just be me and Laney. I would be absolutely trapped!

Jared experiences relationships as a straitjacket. He must be a certain way, otherwise he'll be rejected or abandoned. He has no choice. He can't say "no." He can't speak up about what he feels and what he needs.

For Jared, getting into a relationship is like getting into a car that has no steering wheel or brakes, only a gas pedal. As soon as he closes the door and steps on the gas, he'll be careening down the street without any control, without any way to stop. And the only outcome will be a devastating crash. There is no avoiding it.

But why doesn't Jared have the sense that he can steer? Or the sense that he can say "no" and put on the brakes? It's because he carries a catastrophic belief that every woman will react like his mother—that every woman will show the same disdain, anger, rejection, and potential for abandonment that his mother showed him. And so he carries that fear, even though Laney is saying this is a relationship that's flexible, a relationship in which she can accept some of his limitations. Jared sees Laney as his mother. He sees all relationships, even this one, as a car with no steering wheel and no brakes.

Dr. McKay: Jared, I have a feeling that you expect saying "no" to Laney—telling her "I can't do something, I don't want something" or that you want something very different from what she wants—will end in disaster. I'm curious whether there are other things going on right now in your relationship that we haven't talked about yet—not just what Laney might want from you with her mother. Have you been afraid to tell her your feelings and your needs about any other things, or afraid to tell her that there's something happening that you don't like and would like to stop?

Jared: Laney has this way of probing me—she's very curious about other people and the way they work. And I don't mind engaging in that sort of conversation sometimes. But it can quickly go too far and reach a point where I'm really intensely uncomfortable and I want it to stop.

Dr. McKay: And what would happen if you lived together? What would happen then if Laney was probing you?

Jared: The ability to escape would disappear if we lived together. My private life would be part of a common room rather than an inner sanctum.

Dr. McKay: So if you and Laney lived together, your inner sanctum would be violated.

Jared: When I was a child, I always felt that. My mother actually opened letters I got from my girlfriend and read them before I had a chance to read them. She read them and then banned me from ever seeing the girl again. I mean, that was it! It was my mother's decision, it wasn't mine. It was only when I was away at school that I felt any sense of freedom. That I felt I actually could have a life of my own, that she wasn't overseeing at every juncture. That she wasn't controlling at every juncture.

Dr. McKay: So your expectation is that with Laney, you'll have no privacy—no personal space.

Jared: That's the way it is, isn't it?

Dr. McKay: And if you attempt to live your life with her, she'll invade it whenever she wants to find out what you're doing or thinking.

Jared: That's the thing. When people live together, when they marry, when they merge, there is no self any more. There is no privacy. There is no place to withdraw and refuel, to be by yourself.

Dr. McKay: And what do you think would happen if you said to Laney, "I want this time for myself. I want this room for myself. I want my thoughts here to remain undisturbed"?

Jared: She'd probably feel hurt and give me that hurt look she has sometimes. And I'd feel terribly guilty about it.

Dr. McKay: She'd be hurt and you'd be guilty, and then you'd want to let go and just allow the invasion to happen.

Jared: I hate feeling guilty! I mean, I absolutely hate it.

Dr. McKay: So in the relationship, you'd rather let her invade you than feel guilty.

Jared: Yes.

Dr. McKay: Let me ask you, Laney, right now. Jared's afraid of losing control over his privacy and independence, the integrity of a private space where he can keep his thoughts, his sense of independence and integrity—someplace that's his own. What do you think would happen if he tried to protect such an environment, such a space, in a house where you lived together?

Laney: If I understood Jared right, I think he was speaking metaphorically about an inner place. But whether it's an inner place or an actual physical room, I'd have to say—I'm old enough, I've had enough experience in relationships to realize that that has to be protected. Each person needs their own space. You can't expect to look inside someone and know every part of him or her. It injures a person to do that. There may be some parts of a person that aren't ready to be looked at or exposed to light. Everyone needs their own secret rooms, their own private spaces.

Dr. McKay: So Jared, here again is another bit of evidence that doesn't quite fit with the hypothesis that if you involve yourself with a woman, she will turn out to respond very similarly to your mother. Laney is saying, "I respect your need for privacy—both your inner space and a physical space that's your own." She's saying she knows that's important. And yet this doesn't really seem to fit with the picture you were describing. This is another bit of evidence that Laney may be different. What's happening right now as you hear that?

Jared: I mean, she's a marvelous woman. She really is. I do admire her tremendously.

Dr. McKay: Is she different from your mother? That's the question.

Jared: They're nothing alike—I mean, they're night and day.

Dr. McKay: Will she suffocate you like your mother? Will she control you like your mother? That's the question that we're getting at right now, and we're looking to find out.

Therapist's Overview

Engulfment fear has at its root the fear of self-assertion. The core belief of people who fear engulfment is that if they stand up for themselves—if they fully express their needs and feelings in a relationship—their partner won't tolerate it. He or she will get angry and reject them. The fear of self-assertion starts a chain of events that ends up triggering the impulse to run.

Here's how it works. Individuals who fear engulfment begin a relationship by trying to find out what the other person needs—emotionally, socially, sexually. Then they try to give those things, be those things. In the beginning it feels great. Their new partner loves how caring and attentive they are; appreciates them as a sensitive lover, a generous friend. But there's a problem. The relationship is out of balance. The focus is all on their partner's needs. They've put so much energy into being good—even perfect—that their own needs and feelings have gotten lost.

They start to sense that their true self is missing from the relationship. They have feelings that never get put into words. Things are happening that they don't like, that they wish could be changed. But, because they're afraid of being assertive, they say nothing. It all starts to seem wrong. They feel numb, or bored, or irritated. Underneath it all is a sense of anxiety, a feeling that they can't breathe. They want to get away, to retreat to a place where they have control.

The word "control" is important here, because that's what triggers engulfment fear. The person who fears engulfment is terrified of relinquishing control of their life, giving it to their partner. The relationship is all about satisfying someone else. There's no room for their own feelings and needs, and they suffocate.

Engulfment fear grows from three destructive beliefs:

1. The belief that the other person in your relationship should always come first, the conviction that other people's feelings and desires are more important than your own. Psychologists call this a *subjugation schema*.

2. The tendency to idealize your partner. A person with engulfment issues may see his or her role in life as making sure their partner is protected and happy. They feel it as a reflection of their own personal or moral failure if their partner feels sad or bad. This is the *pedestal trap*.

3. A phenomenon known as *rejection projection*. This is the assumption on the part of the person with engulfment fears that their partner will judge and then leave them. Such an assumption makes the fearful person perpetually vigilant, waiting for the ax to fall. In their own minds, they have to try to figure out what their partner needs and give it to them before the inevitable disaster occurs. The underlying belief of such people is that they're flawed. So the best way to hold onto relationships is to keep themselves safe from criticism, judgment, and rejection by making sure they give far more than they receive.

Engulfment fear is generated by two main patterns in a person's family of origin. The most common is the highly controlling parent. In this scenario, a rigid, micromanaging father or mother evaluates and controls everything. The child's own tastes, preferences, or needs are rarely considered. And if children or adolescents in such families have the temerity to say anything about what they want, they are scolded and criticized until they give up.

A second common pattern that triggers engulfment fear is the dysfunctional parent. In these cases, the parent's behavior is influenced by mental illness, substance abuse, or a compromising medical condition. Once again, there's no room for a child's feelings and needs.

Nobody pays any attention to him or her. Instead, the resources of the entire family are focused on survival, on keeping the dysfunctional parent from complete collapse.

Subjectively, a person struggling with engulfment fear may have no awareness that they are afraid. Instead they notice a shift in their enjoyment of the relationship. Attraction is replaced by irritation, interest by apathy. What once was fun and desirable now seems tiresome, confining. The impulse is to get free, to get away.

How do you determine if changing feelings in a relationship might be influenced by engulfment fear? The following questionnaire may help. If you and your partner take this test, you may both find the results enlightening, and they may serve as a place to start in a discussion of the role of engulfment in your relationship. If your partner is unwilling to fill out the questionnaire, complete it yourself, based on what you know about his or her background and behavior.

Engulfment Questionnaire

1. My life as a child was very controlled by one or both of my parents.

1	2	3	4	5
NOT AT ALL		SOME		A LOT

2. People in my family discouraged or punished me for saying what I felt or wanted.

1	2	3	4	5
NOT AT ALL		SOME		A LOT

3. I feel uncomfortable saying "no" to things my partner wants.

1	2	3	4	5
NOT AT ALL		SOME		A LOT

4. My partner's needs seem more important than mine.

1	2	3	4	5
NOT AT ALL		SOME		A LOT

5. I am uncomfortable expressing my feelings to my partner.

1	2	3	4	5
NOT AT ALL		SOME		A LOT

6. I feel responsible for my partner's needs and happiness.

1	2	3	4	5
NOT AT ALL		SOME		A LOT

7. My job in life is to give my partner what he or she needs.

1	2	3	4	5
NOT AT ALL		SOME		A LOT

8. I reach a point in relationships where I get bored or irritated and need to get away.

1	2	3	4	5
NOT AT ALL		SOME		A LOT

9. I can reach a point in relationships where I feel controlled by my partner's needs.

1	2	3	4	5
NOT AT ALL		SOME		A LOT

10. People are prone to judge and reject you if they don't get what they want.

1	2	3	4	5
NOT AT ALL		SOME		A LOT

11. I reach a point where I can't be myself in relationships.

1	2	3	4	5
NOT AT ALL		SOME		A LOT

12. People with whom I've been in relationships seem uncomfortable when I talk about what I feel or want.

1	2	3	4	5
NOT AT ALL		SOME		A LOT

SCORE _____

If your score on the questionnaire adds up to 36 or more points, then a fear of self-assertion is probably influencing your relationship.

If you filled out the questionnaire for your partner, think about the results as more of an indicator than a prescription—it's very hard for any one human being to know just how another human being feels. That said, it's important for anyone with a fear of self-assertion to learn that they have the right to express their needs and desires. You can and should reassure your partner that, far from rejecting them, you would like to encourage and support them in being more assertive. They need to learn a new lesson—that expressing their needs can result in a positive experience rather than hurt and loss.

Action Plan

The fastest way for a person to overcome engulfment fear is to begin expressing more of his or her wants and experience no negative consequences for doing so (thus taking steps to unlearn the lessons from the past, as explained above). Let your partner know that you really want to know more about his or her wants and needs; and then ask him or her the following questions:

1. Can you tell me about a way you would like to be soothed when you're feeling low?
2. What's your favorite nonsexual way to be touched or caressed?
3. What's the kind of touch that most relaxes you?
4. What are some things you'd enjoy talking about but rarely get to?
5. Is there something you'd enjoy doing sexually?
6. Is there a place you'd like us to go together?
7. What's a fun activity we've never done together that you'd like to try?
8. Is there anything that happens between us that you wish could stop? (It's all right if there's more than one thing. I'll listen.)
9. Is there a way I talk to you that you wish could be different?
10. Are there ways you would like me to express my affection for you?

It's very important for you to be accepting and nonjudgmental when your partner confides in you in this way. He or she is taking a big risk and doing something very scary. Any criticism or scorn on your part, even if only implied, will defeat the purpose of the exercise. The idea is to prove to your partner that assertion of his or her needs is a safe and appropriate thing to do in your relationship.

If your partner's answers begin to scare you—or seem inappropriate to you—you may want to finish the rest of the exercise with the help of a therapist or counselor. Don't express any negative judgments; just stop and say, "I'd like to finish this with you later."

Here's an example of how one of my clients—a forty-two-year-old man—answered the questions when posed by his partner:

1. **Can you tell me about a way you would like to be soothed when you're feeling low?**
    I'd like you to show you're aware of my feelings by putting on some piece of music you know I like but not necessarily asking me to talk about my feelings.

2. **What's your favorite nonsexual way to be touched or caressed?**
   I'd like you to hold me without saying anything or needing to say anything.

3. **What's the kind of touch that most relaxes you?**
   I like having a scalp massage or a neck rub.

4. **What are some things you'd enjoy talking about but rarely get to?**
   I wish we could talk more about politics and social activism. You always look a little bored when I bring up these subjects.

5. **Is there something you'd enjoy doing sexually?**
   I would like to make love somewhere other than our own bed—maybe in the backseat of the car sometime, or out in nature. Or in the kitchen! I'd like you to surprise me sometime by coming out of the bathroom wearing sexy lingerie.

6. **Is there a place you'd like us to go together?**
   I'd like to take a road trip to Alaska together.

7. **What's a fun activity we've never done together that you'd like to try?**
   I've always wanted to try hang gliding.

8. **Is there anything that happens between us that you wish could stop? (It's all right if there's more than one thing. I'll listen.)**
   I hate the way you act when your sister is around. It's like our whole relationship just goes out the window.

9. **Is there a way I talk to you that you wish could be different?**
   Again, the way you talk to me when your sister is around. I really wish you'd be more aware of how you act then—how

your whole attitude to me changes, like I just don't matter to you. Like I'm not even part of your life.

10. **Are there ways you would like me to express my affection for you?**
    I'd like more surprises. I'd love it if you'd show up at the office sometime when I have to work late and bring food or just bring yourself. I'd like it if you'd surprise me sometimes with tickets to something I really want to see.

When a relationship is marked by engulfment fear, a great first step is to encourage your partner to start talking about his or her feelings and needs. Bear in mind, though, that beliefs established in childhood are not easily relinquished. Learning to feel safe can be a long and arduous process.

Just recognizing that the person you love has engulfment issues will go a long way toward sensitizing you to his or her special needs. You can't solve what is, after all, someone else's problem. But you can help create an environment in which your partner feels safe in trying to deal with engulfment fears. It's a tricky business because if you try to micromanage your partner's "recovery" you will only exacerbate his or her anxieties. Learn to back off. Be patient. And be realistic about what's possible. (The final chapter in this book gives clear guidelines about when to give up versus when it makes sense to continue working on a relationship.) It often helps to set goals for the next small step you want to take toward greater commitment. Find a low-pressure way to share this with your partner.

The more openness you can create with a partner who fears engulfment, the safer he or she will feel being close to you and strengthening the bond you share.

---◆---

2

The Fear of Abandonment

Is There a Magic Glue to Make You Stay?

Gary and Sierra provide a perfect illustration of how the fear of abandonment can undermine even the most promising long-term love relationship.

They had been living together for a year when they came to me for counseling, Sierra sporting a conspicuously lovely engagement ring on her left hand. The ring's sapphire stone was an exact match for Sierra's blue eyes. She was dark haired, petite, and well dressed; very tailored in her style and guarded in her emotions.

By contrast, everything was big about Gary—his stature, his hands, his voice, and the feelings he exuded. He gave the sense of being the sort of guy you'd like to have close by in an emergency. He'd be the one in the disaster movie who would be handing the women and children into the lifeboats. His desire to patch things up with Sierra was palpable.

Sierra was the communications manager for a construction firm with projects and offices all over the world. She traveled frequently, and one could tell that she enjoyed this part of her job, which took her to exotic and appealing locales. Kuala Lumpur, Buenos Aires, and Sydney, Australia, were just some of the places she mentioned. Gary fidgeted noticeably while Sierra spoke about her work.

Gary was a contractor, a specialist in remodeling kitchens and bathrooms, whose work never took him more than fifty miles away from home. Although he had a degree in art history, he'd never figured out how to use his degree to make a living. And he liked work-ing with his hands. He liked—and I use his exact words here—"mak-ing things right." He said he found it enormously satisfying to listen to what a client wanted and then to find a way to convert what was, as often as not, a big mess into something attractive and useful. He said he loved the feeling he got when he knew he'd not only solved the client's problem but had been able to envision and execute some-thing even more beautiful than his client had imagined. This was a man who derived a great deal of his satisfaction from other people's approval and would spare no effort to earn it.

Sierra, by her own admission, was not an easy woman to please. She drove herself mercilessly in her job, often working seventeen-hour days that continued after she got home and even longer hours when she traveled. The idea of simply kicking back and relaxing was completely foreign to her. She was a relentless multitasker. She wouldn't chat on the phone without doing something else—folding clothes or some other housekeeping chore—at the same time. When she wasn't at work, she was working out or cleaning her house or improving herself or the things around her in some other way. She listened to language tapes in the car. Before she left on a trip, she would assemble a file folder of *New Yorker* articles she hadn't got-ten around to reading, and she'd read them on the plane. All her pic-tures were in albums. Her fingernails were always tidy, and her bed was always made.

Gary thought of home as a place to relax, not work. Gary worked very hard at his job just like Sierra did. But they had very different ideas about what they wanted to do during their nonwork hours.

Before they'd started living together, they used to meet at a par-ticular upscale bar where the clientele was well educated and young enough not to be dowdy but old enough not to be boring. They'd met there over a spilled glass of zinfandel. They were both sitting at the bar when an overenthusiastic raconteur knocked over his wine. Gary used his own handkerchief to mop up the spill and then picked a splinter of glass out of Sierra's finger.

Gary went to the bar because he enjoyed having a couple of drinks after a long day of physical labor, and he relished the conversations he had with people there. Sierra had taken to stopping at the bar after her daily commute for what she called "eating therapy." The bar's specialty was tapas—small, appetizing portions of Spanish food. Sierra said that she typically found it difficult to eat enough when she was under a lot of stress, but at these times she found she ate more readily in company than when she was alone.

She found Gary's nurturing gesture to be irresistible, even though Gary was a far cry from the type of man Sierra usually dated (dark, slim, elegant, and, more often than not, with an accent of one kind or another). Sierra also tended to choose people who were ultimately unavailable for a long-term relationship—she joked that anyone with more than a one-year visa was out of the running. She loved being in love, and she loved romance and dating and feeling seductive and desirable. But she'd managed never to have a relationship that lasted longer than a year. At thirty-six, she'd begun to wonder whether there wasn't something wrongheaded about her approach to love. That's when Gary picked the splinter of glass out of her hand.

Like Sierra, Gary had also had his share of relationship troubles, although he saw them as things that happened *to* him rather than things he contributed to through his own actions. He had been with his high school sweetheart for ten years, until she surprised him by running off with someone else. And then he was in a ten-year-long marriage with a woman who also surprised him by suddenly announcing she wanted a divorce. He now had joint custody of their eight-year-old daughter. Gary wanted Sierra to be a real mother to his daughter and to help him make a home for her. But things weren't progressing the way he thought they should. Sierra found one excuse after another to postpone their wedding, and they were starting to fight.

Sierra had core abandonment issues that were undermining her prospects for a successful long-term love relationship. It was only in therapy that these issues came to the fore.

Gary and Sierra's Commitment Dialogue

Gary: I just don't understand what's happening with Sierra and me. She says she wants to marry me, but we've already chosen a date for our wedding and then put it off three times. There's always something unavoidable that comes up for her—some kind of emergency at her job or some other reason why a date we've chosen won't work for her. I'm really beginning to wonder whether she wants to get married at all.

Dr. McKay: How does that make you feel?

Gary: Well, I thought we were on this path, a path to a future together. But now I feel like I'm on that path all by myself.

Dr. McKay: So it doesn't seem like Sierra's there with you any more. What you thought you were doing together, you're just doing alone.

Gary: Yeah. And it brings up a lot of stuff for me, because this kind of thing has happened to me before. I thought everything was going along great, and then all of a sudden it ended.

Dr. McKay: So you don't understand why Sierra is pulling away.

Gary: I *don't* understand. We love each other. I mean, I *thought* we loved each other. I thought we had an understanding. It's so scary to suddenly think you might have it all wrong. You start to think it was just an illusion.

Dr. McKay: So right now you need to find out what's going on. Why are you and Sierra fighting more? Why does she keeps postponing your wedding?

Gary: That's why we're here.

Dr. McKay: Let me turn to Sierra for a minute. Sierra, Gary describes some of the things that have changed in your relationship in terms of his feeling like the possibility of marriage is not as close as it once was. He feels like the two of you may be on different pages on this subject. What's happening in this relationship that makes you reluctant to marry?

Sierra: Things aren't going that well in the relationship, or else they haven't been for the last, I don't know, six months? Like Gary mentioned, we really argue a lot. Not so much arguing, but I feel like he's always criticizing me. He doesn't think anything about me is "right." What I do isn't right. My attitude isn't right. I'm not fitting in to some idea he has about me.

Dr. McKay: What does he want you to be that is hard for you to live up to?

Sierra: I guess it's kind of like this maternal earth-mother kind of person who's going to jump in and be a fabulous stepmother to Annie. I don't have a lot of experience with children, and I'm really busy in my job. He has this idea that you just add water and somehow we're going to be this happy family. I don't know, I feel like he's trying to mold me into something. And he's critical and sort of belittling when I don't fit into that mold.

Dr. McKay: So he wants you to be more of a mother to Annie?

Sierra: Yeah.

Dr. McKay: Are there other things that you feel he's asking for that he's disappointed about?

Sierra: Oh, yeah—I think he'd like me to quit my job, frankly. He hasn't said that. But every time I go out of town, he lays a major guilt trip on me about going, that I won't be there for this or that event at Annie's school or her ballet recital . . .

Dr. McKay: So Gary finds you altogether too busy and too committed to your work, and he wants you to be much more oriented to the home and the family. Is that right?

Sierra: I guess so. I guess he'd kind of like me to do all of it: to be this really super-successful person in my work and on the home front, and to be really nurturing, too.

Dr. McKay: Do you feel criticized or somehow not good enough when Gary talks to you about his concerns?

Sierra: Yeah! It really turns me off. It makes me think, "Screw this!" I don't want to be here; I don't want to be listening to this. I want to be doing something really productive. This doesn't feel productive to me. It just feels like he's wearing me down, grinding me down.

Dr. McKay: And then what happens after you two have struggled around one of these issues, around being a mother to Annie or taking more time and investing it in the home, in the relationship, in the family? What happens in the relationship after that?

Sierra: I've tried on a number of occasions to get more into it. I got into this whole idea of making some changes in our house to make it more conducive to being a family gathering place. And I really was trying to talk to him about some issues about Annie and his ex-wife and all this stuff. And he just shut down. He wasn't there for the discussion. He just said something like, "Yeah, whatever!" and he went and watched TV. That's what he does all the time. He's always just turning on the TV. I feel like he turns me off and he turns on the TV.

Dr. McKay: Gary, let me ask you a question. Do you feel a need for Sierra to be some things that at the moment she isn't—to be more involved with Annie, to be more involved in the home, to be perhaps less a professional person and more someone who really puts her energy into the relationships and the people in her life?

Gary: I get so frustrated. It hurts me so much to see what she's doing to herself. I don't know if I mentioned this to you before, but, before I knew Sierra, she had a bout with colon cancer. It really was a significant event in her life, and I feel like she's running. She's running from this stuff rather than stopping and taking care of herself. I feel like what I want for Sierra is what's right for *her*. And I know it's going to be right for us as a couple and as a family.

Dr. McKay: And when Sierra doesn't do what you think is right for her, what's right for the family, what happens to you then?

Gary: I feel so thwarted. I love this woman, and I'm trying so hard to do what's right, to make things right. I really have this vision of how it could be, and I know it could be that way. And she won't go there!

Dr. McKay: And then do you retreat? Do you shut down? What happens?

Gary: I feel frustrated. And sometimes I get angry.

Dr. McKay: And what do you do with that anger? What happens?

Gary: There's nothing to do. I mean, what am I going to do?

Dr. McKay: So what actually happens? What actually occurs in terms of your behavior, and what happens between you?

Gary: I've just got to distract myself. I've just got to get out of that place and go someplace. So I turn on the tube and have a beer or whatever. I just can't be in that place. It's too painful.

Dr. McKay: It's too painful when Sierra can't agree to the things you're asking her to be. You just kind of pull back and try to get to a safe place where you can cope and manage.

Gary: Maybe it's where I won't hurt her. Sometimes I feel so frustrated, I just . . .

Dr. McKay: You're afraid of lashing out?

Gary: Yeah, I am.

Dr. McKay: Sierra, let me ask you, when Gary retreats during an argument and avoids confronting you or being confronted, how does that make you feel?

Sierra: I just feel wrong. I mean, look at Gary. Look at him! He's Mr. Sunshine. He's Mr. Wonderful. And I know he loves me. But I can't be what he wants me to be. I just can't—there's something wrong with me.

Dr. McKay: And when you can't be what he wants you to be, what's the feeling that comes up inside?

Sierra: It hurts.

Dr. McKay: And when he withdraws and watches TV?

Sierra: I just feel like he's saying, "Screw this. Screw you. You're not worth my time."

Sierra is in a lot of pain. Gary is, too. But while he seems to pull back from confrontations with Sierra, he's not pulling back from the relationship.

Sierra is really ambivalent now. She feels criticized; she feels that Gary is saying that she's not good enough. But there's something deeper than that. There's something that's really frightening her. And whatever it is that's frightening her is driving her reactions in this relationship.

It's certainly painful to feel you're not everything your partner wants you to be. But Sierra is running. She's avoiding. And I have to get her to dig up what it is she's running away from, what's at the root of her fear.

Dr. McKay: Sierra, when Gary criticizes you, and you feel bad about yourself, there's also a fear there. There's something that's scaring you. Can you feel that fear? Are you aware of it right now?

Sierra: I know there's something almost physical I feel.

Dr. McKay: What is that feeling? What happens in your body when Gary's criticizing, or when he's just sitting watching the television, shut down and distanced?

Sierra: Honestly, it's like I kind of have trouble breathing, and I can hear my heart pounding. It's like a physical fear about something. It's not rational, but it's really vivid.

Dr. McKay: So you're afraid.

Sierra: Yeah. I mean, he's just watching television. It shouldn't be a scary thing. But there's something . . . Maybe I feel that anger he was talking about underneath it.

Dr. McKay: What's going to happen, Sierra? What do you think is going to happen? Not five minutes away, not ten minutes away, not ten days away. But when that fear comes up, what are you afraid is going to happen with you and Gary?

Sierra: (*crying now*) I think he's going to give up on me.

Dr. McKay: He's going to leave.

Sierra: Yeah, he's going to withdraw all his love, and he's going to decide I'm not worth it. He's just going to walk away.

What we're learning now about Sierra is something extraordinarily important. Gary's criticism and Gary's withdrawal are much bigger for her than the simple fights and disagreements that all couples have. She reacts to these as harbingers of abandonment; she's convinced he's going to leave her. Gary's ways of coping with confrontation, criticism followed by withdrawal, are indications for Sierra that the end is near.

We need to find out more about the origin of Sierra's fear. Where does it come from? It wouldn't seem to be only about Sierra and Gary. There's some history here that's influencing the interactions between these two.

Dr. McKay: Sierra, is this the first time you've ever felt this fear? Or is it something you recognize from other times in your life?

Sierra: I guess this is the first relationship I've allowed to get this far. Usually I end them first. I end them myself.

Dr. McKay: You end them yourself because . . . ?

Sierra: I don't want them to leave me. The longer a relationship goes on, the more nervous I get. I don't want to become dependent on something that's just going to fall apart anyway.

Dr. McKay: So when this fear comes up, in the past you've drawn a line and put an end to that relationship because the idea of being abandoned is so scary.

Sierra: I'd rather be in control of it. At least, when I'm leaving, I'm making the decision, and I'm not so vulnerable! That's the scary thing for me, the sense that . . .

Dr. McKay: Just waiting for the ax to fall. Waiting for the end to come.

Sierra: Yes! Knowing it's going to happen!

Dr. McKay: So he's criticizing things about how you mother and the kind of energy you bring to the family. And it feels like those criticisms are the beginning of what inevitably will lead to losing him, losing the relationship, but also really being left and abandoned.

Sierra: It's like, what I am isn't right somehow. He's got to make things right. He wants to remodel me! And I just feel like I can't go there. I can't do that!

Dr. McKay: And so in the past when you felt this way, you've chosen to leave the relationship. When you get scared and feel like your partner is criticizing the way you are and how you do things . . . In the past what you've done is you left before you could be abandoned. Does that sound right, Sierra?

Sierra: Yeah. I don't want to count on any kind of future together, because sooner or later . . .

Dr. McKay: Gary, let me ask you something. Did you know how scary it was for Sierra when you expressed some of those concerns and criticisms about how she is with Annie, how she is at home, the time and energy she brings to the home? Were you aware how that affects her?

Gary: No, I didn't know she was scared. I thought she was angry with me. I didn't know she was scared.

Dr. McKay: Okay, so you were reading anger, and sometimes she might be somewhat angry. But really what's underneath is the fear that your criticisms are the first step down a path to abandonment.

Gary: Honestly, I thought it was the opposite. I felt like she was abandoning me!

Dr. McKay: It felt very different to you.

Gary: Totally different!

Dr. McKay: I think we're going to need to explore—you and I, Gary—what we can do to make Sierra feel safer in this relationship. But let's learn a little bit more about the fear. Sierra, in the past you've felt this fear with other relationships, other boyfriends. Did they want you to be something you're not, or have an agenda for you, or a picture of who you should be—some ideal Sierra that you couldn't quite live up to?

Sierra: Well, I never really let a love affair get beyond the romantic phase. I hate it when reality sets in, when they see you're not who they wanted you to be. Because then they withdraw all their warmth, all their love, all that attention—everything you worked for. They're gone. It's over.

Dr. McKay: When did that happen to you, Sierra?

Sierra: It's hard to talk about.

Dr. McKay: This is so scary and so painful. I know at some point in your life this has happened to you.

Sierra: (*crying*) I guess, you know, my dad was . . . I was his favorite. And he just had so many dreams for me. He was an English teacher, and then he became a school principal. And he thought I was going to follow the same path. But I didn't want to! I felt like I couldn't live up to what he wanted me to be. I really tried. I tried so hard . . .

Dr. McKay: What happened then? What happened when you weren't the daughter he wanted you to be?

Sierra: I was fourteen. I was just starting high school, and I had a boyfriend, my first boyfriend. My dad was just so contemptuous. I remember once, I put on some makeup. I was going to my first dance. And he was so critical! He said I looked like a prostitute. He said I wasn't serious, that I wasn't a serious person. And after that . . .

Dr. McKay: So instead of being perfect and special and being everything he ever dreamed you could be, you were failing him.

Sierra: I was just an adolescent girl. I was just doing what girls do, and he wasn't there for me. He was never there for me after that. That was *it*. He just withdrew more and more, mostly into his work. He hardly paid attention to me anymore after that.

Dr. McKay: So, Sierra, it felt like you lost your father when you were fourteen?

Sierra: Yeah.

Dr. McKay: And you lost him because you weren't what he wanted you to be. You weren't the model student, the principal's star pupil, who was going to be a school principal herself one day—

Sierra: Superintendent of Schools, more like. When I was little, he'd say, "You're going to be a bright light. You're going to shine that light all over this state."

Dr. McKay: And then when you weren't that light, not quite the way he wanted—when he found that you were interested in boys as well as studying—suddenly you were on the wrong side of all of his dreams. You weren't "the one."

Sierra: He didn't have any time for me after that. And he couldn't even see it, when I did shine my light, when I did do good things. When I did my first marketing campaign in business school, I sent it to him. And then, when I was visiting my parents later, I saw he'd never even opened the packet. I couldn't believe it.

Dr. McKay: You never want to feel that again, do you? You never want to go through that again, that sense of losing someone's love, of not being enough for them. Not being the one they wanted.

We've learned something very important here. We know now what scares Sierra so much in her relationship with Gary. She fears a reenactment of the extraordinary emotional loss she felt at the age of fourteen, when a father who had idealized and elevated her, turned his back on her, abandoning her emotionally.

In a moment, we will want to clarify exactly how Sierra's experience with her father has influenced her feelings with Gary and how she's coped with the fear that Gary, like her father, will decide she's not good enough and leave.

Dr. McKay: Sierra, when Gary tells you that he wants you to be more of a mother to Annie, more involved in the home, more involved with him, and he becomes disappointed and angry, and finally withdraws in front of the television, you feel afraid. And you feel afraid that you've entered a time warp, that you're reliving your life with your father and that you'll be rejected and hurt and abandoned in the same way you were at fourteen. And when you get scared that Gary, like your father, has found some flaw in you that he can't accept, what do you do then? How do you cope with that anxiety, that fear?

Sierra: I guess I just keep busy. I try to plunge into work or some project at home or working out. I just try to keep going, because I don't want to stand still. I don't want to stand still and feel that feeling.

Dr. McKay: So you get busy. You get involved in your work. You get involved in projects. So that's one way you cope. Are there other ways?

Sierra: I think about leaving.

Dr. McKay: Leaving so you can get away from this fear?

Sierra: Yeah.

Dr. McKay: And is this why you keep putting off the wedding?

Sierra: It feels like a trap. I just don't want to put myself in a position where I'm tied to someone. Where I depend on him and . . .

Dr. McKay: And what?

Sierra: And he's gone.

Dr. McKay: Walks out?

Sierra: Emotionally, maybe. The thing with Annie . . . It's complicated. I have a little sister, and when my dad decided I wasn't worth the effort anymore, he focused all his attention on her instead. Gary is a wonderful father. It's a wonderful thing, it's a beautiful thing, the way Gary loves Annie, but . . .

Dr. McKay: So the fear is that Gary will take the energy and love he has for you and pour it into his daughter and leave you out.

Sierra: (*crying*) There won't be any left for me.

Dr. McKay: I understand.

In the second phase, we begin to look at what Gary and Sierra can do together to deal with this terrible fear of abandonment that's keeping Sierra so ambivalent, so uncertain.

Dr. McKay: Gary, let me ask you something. Sierra is very scared. When you criticize her, and you ask her to be more attentive to Annie or more attentive to your life at home, I'm sure you had no idea that, for her, that had a huge significance. It was much more than just a request. It was something that meant the beginning of an enormous, overwhelming loss on her end. That's how she read it. And then when you got kind of angry and a little bit disgusted with things not changing, and withdrew into the television, her anxiety got even greater, because your actions seemed to justify her fear.

Gary: I had no idea! Sierra, I'm really sorry. I didn't know. I didn't understand. Is there something I can do so you don't go to that place?

Dr. McKay: That's a good question, Gary, and it's the most important thing we can look at right now. Because the fear Sierra feels when she thinks she's about to be abandoned, when she thinks she's about to relive her father's emotional abandonment, is making her want to run. And she actually did run from some of those other relationships, when it felt like she wasn't quite living up to whatever they expected. It makes her want to run, so that she can avoid being abandoned.

Gary: Sierra, I love you. I want us to share our lives. I want you to feel safe with me. I want to be the guy you can count on, the guy you know will always be there for you. I will always be there for you, Sierra.

Dr. McKay: Sierra, as you're listening to Gary, what's happening inside of you right now?

Sierra: It's hard to believe. (*Crying, she speaks in barely a whisper.*) It's hard to believe.

Dr. McKay: Those are words you want to believe, but you're not sure that you can count on their really being true?

Sierra: It's hard to believe that anyone could love me so much.

Dr. McKay: Let me ask you something, Sierra, and this is really important, because it will allow us to begin this next phase of work. What is it that you need from Gary so that you can feel safer in this relationship, so that you can feel that this relationship is not a replication of your life with your father?

Sierra: I think one of the things I need is to go more slowly, so I don't have to get in that place where I feel so scared. I think I need him to be a little more patient with me, because it's not easy.

Now, Sierra is asking for something that's really important, but she's asking in generalities. She's asking for an attitude shift that may be very hard for Gary to achieve or even recognize. So now we need to get more specific. We need to turn the general into the particular and find out what Gary can do at particular moments when Sierra is most afraid, to give her the sense of safety that she never had with her father.

Dr. McKay: Sierra, I'm wondering whether you could give Gary a signal when you're getting scared, when something has made you scared that you're losing him, that you're losing all that you have together?

Sierra: You mean, like kind of throw up a red flag?

Dr. McKay: Yeah.

Sierra: I think I could do that if we could agree on something, like a word . . .

Dr. McKay: What word would you like to use to let Gary know that you've gotten into that really scared place?

Sierra: (*crying*) Maybe, "Time out!"

Dr. McKay: Okay. So if you said, "Time out!" to Gary, that would mean, "I'm really scared, and I need to stop everything we're talking about, and I just need . . ."

Sierra: I need to slow it down, and I need him to be there with me, and I need to know that he's not going to go, that he's going to stay with me while I'm feeling this.

Dr. McKay: Gary, let me ask you a question. If Sierra said, "Time out!" to you, which means, "I'm getting scared that I'm going down the same emotional road I went down with my father—I'm scared I'm going to be left, I'm scared I'm going to be abandoned." If she said, "Time out!" would you be able to stop the conversation in its tracks, whatever the concern was, whatever was upsetting you? Could you be there for her then and let her know that you're not leaving her?

Gary: I absolutely could commit to that.

Dr. McKay: So, step one then, and something that is going to be tremendously important in your relationship, is to be able to signal—wave a flag when that fear has gotten really strong—and to be able to ask for a response from Gary that gives you some feeling of reassurance and support that all of those scary things that happened with your father are not going to happen again in this relationship.

Sierra: Do I have to wait until it gets really strong, or can I do it when I start to feel the feelings?

Dr. McKay: I think it would be good to signal Gary when the feelings start and not wait until they are overwhelming, because when they are overwhelming, then *you* want to run away.

Sierra: Yeah, I do.

Dr. McKay: So now we have a signal, and we have something that Gary can do to help you not go down that road to fear and wanting to run. But there's more we need to do. When Gary is concerned about something, when there's something he wants to ask you or some change he wants to make in the relationship or to the patterns of your life, how can he do it in a way that won't make you want to run? Do you have some suggestions for Gary?

Sierra: Well, maybe if he could kind of preface it by saying, "This isn't a deal-breaker," or saying something like . . .

Dr. McKay: "I'm not going anywhere"?

Sierra: Yeah.

Dr. McKay: So what would you like to hear Gary say as he starts to talk about something he'd like to change? What is it you need to hear him say so that the anxiety, the fear that he's going to leave you—What would feel good to hear him say? What's the first thing that pops into your mind?

Sierra: Maybe, "I'm here for you."

Dr. McKay: Gary, is that something you could say to Sierra when something concerns you, when there's something you'd like to change in the relationship?

Gary: Yeah, I could say that. It seems like a good thing to say.

Dr. McKay: Okay. So when you're expressing a need for something that you'd like to change, you could start by saying, "Sierra, I'm here for you." And then you could begin to talk about what you want to be different. And if Sierra starts to get scared, she could say, "Time out!" and you would reassure her that you aren't leaving.

Sierra: Yes.

Dr. McKay: Okay. Those are two important things we can do to change the kind of fear that Sierra has been struggling with.

There's another important issue that remains unaddressed, and that's when Gary withdraws into the TV, when he becomes angry and feels helpless, having given up hope that he can change Sierra, and he just retreats and checks out of the relationship. This, too, is a signal to Sierra that she is in danger, that abandonment could be imminent. We need to address this so that both Gary and Sierra have a way of handling his withdrawal that isn't damaging and doesn't trigger overwhelming anxiety.

Dr. McKay: Sierra, you've talked about Gary's time in front of the television. And, Gary, you've talked about that experience as something that follows a lot of frustration and maybe anger, trying to make changes in this relationship and feeling like you're running up against a brick wall, like nothing you say or do can make a difference, and finally just giving up and retreating to the solace of watching TV. I want to see if we can figure out what we can do at those moments when you have given up and retreated, and Sierra is experiencing that as a very scary thing, something that's again a harbinger of loss for her. Sierra, I'm wondering, if you were watching Gary during one of those phases, when it seems like he's shut down, pulled away, and distracted, is there something you could say, or some signal you could give, that would let him know that that's scaring you, that it's really hard for you?

Sierra: I don't think I really need to tell Gary anything at this point. I need to ask him to express what's going on with him.

Dr. McKay: So when Gary is kind of shut down, and you're getting scared that he's withdrawing and leaving in some way, what you'd like to do is find out what is happening, what's going on inside of him.

Sierra: What I don't like is that sense that he checks out, that it's not worth it for him to even talk to me.

Dr. McKay: You said you need to ask him a question.

Sierra: I need to ask him what he's feeling, what's going on.

Dr. McKay: Gary, is that something that you'd be willing to do? Could you talk with Sierra if she asked you what you were feeling during one of those times when you've withdrawn?

Gary: Well, if she can deal with it that I'm feeling some strong emotions.

Dr. McKay: You talked before about feeling angry.

Gary: Yeah.

Dr. McKay: Feeling disappointed and stuck.

Gary: Yeah. Can she can deal with that?

Dr. McKay: How can you say it so that she *can* deal with it?

Gary: Maybe I can say that thing: "Sierra, I'm here for you."

Dr. McKay: Okay. Would that help you if Gary started by saying "Sierra, I'm here for you"?

Sierra: Yeah, I think it might.

Dr. McKay: What happens if it gets too scary, too overwhelming?

Sierra: For me? Then I guess I'd say, "Time out."

Dr. McKay: And would you be willing to stop for a while and let her know that you're there for her, Gary?

Gary: Of course I would.

Dr. McKay: So now we have a beginning plan for how to manage those moments when it feels like Gary is withdrawn, and withdrawn in a way that's scary to you, Sierra. And you can ask him what's happening, what's going on, what he's feeling. And Gary will start by saying "Sierra, I'm here for you, and here's what I'm feeling." And if you get scared or overwhelmed, you'll say, "Time out." Is that a plan the two of you would be willing to try out for the next week?

Gary: Yeah.

Sierra: I think so.

Dr. McKay: Something that's very important now is to look at some of Gary's feelings about when you, Sierra, retreat into your work and get involved in a lot of personal tasks and interests. Sometimes that's related to your feelings of wanting to run away, of feeling scared that Gary, like your father, is getting ready to reject you. And you're retreating to a safe place where you can deal with your own experience and your own interests and your own career. But sometimes you may just be, like lots of people, involved not because you're afraid but because your work is interesting and engaging. But when Gary is starting to feel left out, when he's starting to feel disappointed, I'm wondering how he can talk with you about that, and let you know, so that it doesn't set off that fear, and doesn't set off retreat, but is something the two of you can work with.

Therapist's Overview

The fear of abandonment is a deep and compelling anxiety, usually stemming from parental abandonment or rejection during childhood or adolescence. While this fear often goes unrecognized—masquerading as boredom, anger, or disconnection, among other things—abandonment fear can permeate every aspect of your life, dramatically limiting your options and diminishing your potential for happiness.

Fear of abandonment can trigger either of two reactions—the desire to cling or the desire to run.

People who anticipate rejection and loss, and then hang on for dear life, rarely have commitment problems. Their fear of abandonment contributes to their ability to stay in a long-term relationship. Gary, in the foregoing therapy dialogue, is an example of someone who might have abandonment issues but deals with them by hanging on hard to whatever relationship he's in. If the relationship comes to an end, it's always the other person who ends it.

Many people who fear abandonment, people like Sierra, tend to be "runners" rather than "clingers." They are so frightened of loss that they leave first, before they can be rejected. These are the individuals most likely to have problems with commitment.

There are many ways to run. Some people simply shut down all feelings of love or affection. Others take refuge in working too much, in sudden new interests or lovers. Others become angry, forcing wedges of hurt and resentment into the relationship. Still others do what Sierra reported doing in all her previous relationships: they end things preemptively, before they themselves can be left.

Whatever form running takes, the underlying, often unconscious, fear is the same: that a partner will stop loving, stop caring, and leave.

Different triggers can set off abandonment fears. Realizing that one has started to depend on another person can do it. The more someone acknowledges their need for another person, the more vulnerable to rejection he or she feels.

Criticism can trigger the fear, particularly if the person involved had a critical parent. For Sierra, criticism throws her back to those painful days when her father decided she wasn't doing well enough in school and started pushing her away emotionally. Criticism is a signal for her that rejection and loss are imminent. So she runs to a variety of work and personal commitments that distance her from Gary and reduce her levels of anxiety about being abandoned again.

Sometimes abandonment fear is triggered by inattentiveness. You are late or distracted, busy or frequently away. Perhaps you've asked your partner for more space or time alone or you've said "no" to things that feel vitally important to him or her. All of these can stoke your partner's fear that you don't care, that you are about to leave.

Another trigger for abandonment feelings, paradoxically, can be a sudden new closeness in a relationship. Perhaps you and your partner have shared intimate secrets and vulnerabilities have been exposed. Now your partner is feeling the danger of starting to depend on you. Such feelings can be extremely scary to someone who has carefully guarded their ability to thrive on their own. What if you decide to pull away? Your partner's dependence on you leaves him or her terribly exposed to the possibility of feeling pain if you leave.

Perhaps the saddest of all the triggers for abandonment fear is authentic love. For some people—particularly those who've known little love in childhood—the experience of being loved, valued, and admired is terrifying. All their alarm bells go off. Such individuals respond to being loved with a dark logic that goes like this: "You say you love me, but I'm not loveable. Therefore, (1) you don't know me, (2) you're lying, or (3) something's wrong with you. Therefore, I'm in danger, because I will eventually lose the good feeling I have now of being loved by you."

When fear of abandonment lies at the root of a commitment struggle, the first step is to make visible the hidden triggers of your partner's fears. Your partner has to encounter the fear, to see it and find words to describe it, so that you can both take steps to reduce the power it has over your relationship.

The following exercises may be helpful in uncovering buried fears of abandonment and recognizing the situations that serve as emotional triggers for these fears. Ask your partner to fill out the questionnaire that follows. If he or she doesn't feel willing or ready to explore this issue, try filling out the questionnaire from your partner's point of view, to the best of your ability. If you suspect that the fear of abandonment may be an underlying issue for your partner, the questionnaire may help clarify what the triggers are. This knowledge may help you, in turn, be more sensitive to those triggers when they arise.

Worksheet 1

What do you typically feel when . . .

1. Your partner is too busy to be with you?
2. Your partner criticizes you?
3. Your partner cancels plans you looked forward to?
4. You and your partner share deep feelings, secrets, or experiences that are usually difficult to talk about?
5. Your partner is away for a while?
6. You notice someone is attracted to your partner?
7. You notice the ways you depend on your partner?
8. Your partner expresses love or admiration for you?
9. Your partner expresses interest in or admiration for another?
10. Your partner wants to be alone?

Take note of which of the above situations elicit worry or anxiety. These may be the triggers for abandonment fear in your relationship.

Regardless of whether your partner is willing or available to answer the questions in Worksheet 1, fill out the following questionnaire by yourself.

Worksheet 2

What does your partner do or say when . . .

1. You are too busy to be with him or her?
2. You criticize him or her?
3. You cancel plans for something he or she was anticipating with pleasure?
4. You and your partner share deep feelings, secrets, or experiences that are hard to talk about?
5. You are away for a while?
6. He or she notices that someone is attracted to you?

7. He or she has to depend on you for something?
8. You express love or admiration for your partner?
9. You express interest in or admiration for another?
10. You want to be alone?

Notice how many of the above situations elicited an argument or distancing or withdrawal behavior. Reactions that typically create emotional or physical distance may have their genesis in abandonment fear.

The following exercise, the Couple Interview, is an opportunity to explore each other's feelings and reactions surrounding abandonment issues and to create an action plan. When discussing each of the questions, be careful not to interrupt each other. Don't argue or debate about each other's feelings. Instead, summarize in your own words what your partner tells you—simply, clearly, and without comment or judgment.

Couple Interview

The following key questions can help you explore abandonment anxiety as an individual or a couple. You can write responses to each question, or, as partners, you can use the questions as a starting point for a discussion about your feelings and experiences.

1. If you have experienced abandonment in the past—by a parent, sibling, friend, or lover—describe its emotional impact.
2. If your partner decided to end your current relationship, how would the loss affect you emotionally? Why do you think the loss would affect you this way?
3. How often do you find yourself feeling anxiety about losing your relationship? How strong at times does that anxiety become?
4. What experiences in this relationship intensify your anxiety about loss or abandonment? Describe each experience in a way your partner will understand.

5. How did you cope in past relationships when your fear of loss or abandonment was triggered? How do you respond now when fears of loss are triggered? How do you protect yourself from the feelings described in question #2?
6. How might you tell your partner that your fear of loss or abandonment has been triggered?
7. How might your partner reassure you if your fear has been activated?
8. What action might you as partners take to soothe the fear, once it's been triggered? List as many actions as you can think of. Could any of these responses help replace some of your old ways of coping (see question #5)?

Generally, the fear of abandonment diminishes with time. As trust builds, the fear slowly subsides over months and years. However, there are exceptions. High-conflict relationships that are marked by threats or sudden withdrawals may never offer enough safety for abandonment fears to heal. The relationship may endure for years, but the fearful partner is likely always to have one foot outside the door. If you are struggling in a high-conflict relationship, the best remedy is communication skills training—usually with a good couple's therapist.

3

---◆---

The Shame Factor

You Won't Love Me Anymore if You See the Real Me

J acklyn, at the age of thirty-eight, had the sort of job most people can only dream of. A self-employed executive coach, she had managed to become an indispensable confidante and mentor to several of the country's highest-profile CEOs. Jet-setting with the best of them but always remaining behind the scenes, Jacklyn gave her personal life about the same amount of attention she paid to her wardrobe and personal grooming—enough to look good, feel good, and not give her any problems.

In the year and a half before she contacted me, she'd been dating Todd, the thirty-four-year-old pilot of one of her client's corporate jets. Todd was as handsome as a model in a magazine ad, bright, kind, and lots of fun. The trouble was, according to Jacklyn, that he was in love with her. He was "pestering" her (as Jacklyn put it) for a kind of closeness she didn't want to be bothered with. He wanted to live together; she just wanted to play together.

Todd had a chip on his shoulder about being a hired hand in uniform while Jacklyn was wearing cocktail dresses and sipping martinis with his boss, who hung on her every word. Sure, his boss put his life in Todd's hands by letting him fly the plane, but Jacklyn was the puppeteer who was pulling everybody's strings, including Todd's.

She was used to having the high and mighty treating her suggestions as scripture. Todd didn't take kindly, though, to being bossed around, at least not when he was out of uniform. He kept trying to break through Jacklyn's diamond-hard veneer, without any luck at all. He wanted to share secrets, talk about their childhood memories, and make plans for the future. Her idea of being intimate was to ask for a foot rub.

Todd wanted to be her friend, not just her good-time guy. He knew she needed a friend. He saw something hidden in her, but only at moments when she didn't realize he was watching her—when she was sleeping or looking at herself in the mirror. He saw someone who, despite all the carefree outer trappings, seemed desperately unhappy and alone. But the more Todd tried to be there for Jacklyn—to draw her out and get closer to her—the more energetically she pushed him away. It was all starting to get old.

Neither of them was ready to call it quits on the relationship. Todd was very much in love, and Jacklyn thought Todd would be the perfect boyfriend if only he'd lighten up a little. Both of them were upset that they just couldn't seem to agree about how to be happy together.

That's when they came to see me.

Jacklyn and Todd's Commitment Dialogue

Jacklyn: Todd's been really complaining about things. I thought it would be a good idea to come in, lay things out on the table, and get them taken care of so we can get on with our lives.

Dr. McKay: Is that how you see it, Todd?

Todd: I don't know. It might be a good idea to sort this out with another person. I wanted us to live together.

Dr. McKay: You'd like the relationship to take a step forward, go up to the next level. Jacklyn, how do you feel about that?

Jacklyn: I think Todd's terrific. We have a fabulous relationship. And I don't want to blow it. I don't want to change it either.

Dr. McKay: Listening to Jacklyn, do you see the relationship the same way?

Todd: The great parts about this relationship are really great—the laughs, the fun. But Jacklyn's unwillingness to move forward is wrecking it for me. I want more. We don't *really* talk. Whenever I try to get Jackie to talk, it's like she goes somewhere else. She's not there anymore.

Dr. McKay: Todd, how do you make sense of Jacklyn's reluctance to move in? What do you think that means?

Todd: That maybe she's kind of holding out for somebody who's more in her league. It's like we move in different circles. You know, I'm the guy up in the cockpit with the uniform on. I'm the guy opening the door while they all file out to the party.

Dr. McKay: So it feels like maybe you're not good enough for Jacklyn, is that the feeling?

Todd: That's the way it feels sometimes.

Dr. McKay: You're working class, you're the help—

Todd: I'm the help. She likes me; she has a good time with me. I'm her boyfriend; but I'm not somebody she wants to do something permanent with. I'm not her guy for the long haul; I'm not a potential partner. But I know we could be that for each other. Or, at least, that's what I'd like us to be for each other . . .

Dr. McKay: Now, Jacklyn, let me ask you. Todd's concerned about this issue, about living together, for one thing, and doesn't know whether that's going to happen or not. And we've learned from him that he has some theories about why it might not be happening. What's your take on this?

Jacklyn: Totally different! It has nothing to do with social class or uniforms or hired help or anything like that. I mean—hey! I love our relationship. It's the best relationship I've ever had. Todd's a fabulous guy. I think he's totally wrong about this. It's just that I'm not ready for it. I'm not ready for something more permanent with anybody! It's not Todd; it's just me. I really love him. I can't imagine loving anyone more than I love Todd.

Dr. McKay: And yet there's something in you that resists the idea of taking that step toward commitment.

Jacklyn: I don't know if I'm resisting it, Dr. McKay. You know, it's just not where I am right now. It's not a place where I want to be. I'm really happy where we are. We have a great time together, a wonderful time, and a wonderful life.

Dr. McKay: What do you think would happen if you did take that step, if you took a step toward that next level of commitment and lived together?

Jacklyn: It doesn't really bear talking about, because it's not going to happen. It's not where I am. It's not where I want to be right now.

Dr. McKay: I understand that. I understand that you're not feeling ready at all. But I guess what I'm wondering is, Jacklyn, what does it feel like when you imagine that life with Todd? The two of you waking up together every day, coming home to each other every day. Sharing meals, sharing tasks, sharing chores in an apartment or a house. When you imagine that life, what does that feel like?

Jacklyn: It feels like somebody else's life! It doesn't feel like my life. It doesn't feel like Todd's life. I mean, we live this pretty wild life. We're traveling all over the place, all the time. Last year I went overseas a dozen times!

Jacklyn is stonewalling me. Todd complained earlier that Jacklyn doesn't like to talk about things that would deepen their relationship. Now she's resisting my questions; she won't directly answer them.

When people seem afraid to open themselves up, I suspect they may have an underlying fear that something is wrong inside, that something terribly shameful would be revealed if they let themselves be seen.

Dr. McKay: You know, I'm going to ask you something, and I'm going to ask you to think a little bit about it before you answer—

not to give the first answer that occurs to you. I'm wondering what it is you don't want Todd to know about you.

Jacklyn: Why do you think there's something I don't want Todd to know about me?

Dr. McKay: Well, I might be completely wrong. But I'd like you to just consider it for a moment. If there *was* something you really didn't want Todd to know about you, what would that be?

Jacklyn: I thought we were here to talk about Todd's unhappiness with this whole thing. I'm happy with the way things are!

Dr. McKay: We're certainly here to talk about how Todd feels, but I'm interested in how you feel, too. And we need to look at the relationship as a whole. And what's happening between you is that there's a struggle over commitment and, below that, a struggle over how close you and Todd can be in this relationship and still feel safe. So I'm wondering, if you gave it a little bit of thought, are there some things that would be hard to have Todd know about? I'm not asking you to tell me what they are just yet.

Jacklyn: Well, I'm just like anyone else. There are a lot of things that I don't want anybody to know about. There are lots of things that one keeps to oneself that aren't for public consumption. It's just stuff you keep under wraps a little bit. It's part of the mystique. It's part of, you know, being a person out in public.

Dr. McKay: How do you suppose Todd might feel if he knew the really private things about you? How would you feel knowing that he knew those things?

Jacklyn: I'd feel really violated.

Dr. McKay: Okay. Violated. Like someone had really exposed you in some terrible way.

Jacklyn: I don't really like the direction this is taking. I don't like your use of that word.

Dr. McKay: The word "exposed"?

Jacklyn: No, "violated."

Dr. McKay: Hmm.

Jacklyn: I don't understand the direction you're taking here, Dr. McKay. It doesn't seem productive to me.

Dr. McKay: It's a hard thing to talk about.

Jacklyn: What is?

Dr. McKay: The things that we don't want others to know.

Jacklyn: Look—everybody has to have their private places, their privacy! You know, you spend time in the morning getting ready to see the world. Putting on your face. You don't want to do that out on the public streets instead of in your bathroom. It's just not appropriate! It's not appropriate to share some things. I don't go for this idea that we're just, you know, like open books and everybody gets to know everything about us. That's not the way it is. And the work I do is all about the message. I want to stay on message—*my* message of who I am. I want to be the one controlling the information that goes out.

Dr. McKay: I think I understand how you feel. You've built a successful career. You're someone who advises people how to be effective in this world. You move easily among people who are competent, gifted, and talented, and you feel good about what you do. And you don't want to have anyone see what lies beneath your public self.

Jacklyn: You know, it's not so much that my clients are gifted and talented. That's the way it looks, because people like me make it look that way. These guys aren't any smarter than anybody else. They've just got a lot of money and they've got a lot of power. And they've got smart people running the show behind the scenes. And that's what *I* do. I run the show behind the scenes. I stay in control of what goes out there, what the public perceives, what's projected, and what's kept behind closed doors.

Dr. McKay: That makes sense. And I bet they would be a whole lot less effective without you.

Jacklyn: If the public knew what I know about my clients, no one would put any trust in them. They'd be reviled. They'd be drummed out of their positions. They'd be in jail.

Dr. McKay: I kind of want to go back to that question about what might happen if you and Todd were closer. If the two of you shared more. What it is that he might see or learn about you.

Jacklyn: I'm not really one of those people who thinks it's nice to go to the bathroom in front of each other and floss your teeth in front of the other person. I kind of liked the way it was in Victorian times when people lived in these grand houses, and they only saw each other fully dressed, or when they were ready to go to bed together. It was much more romantic that way. I mean, why should we see each other so closely?

Dr. McKay: I understand what you're saying—that we live in an era when perhaps people are more open than you're comfortable with and maybe more open than they should be. But I guess I'm still wondering what might be scary for you to share with Todd. What might you not want Todd to know about?

Jacklyn: It's not so much I don't want Todd to know about it. It's just, I don't like thinking about this stuff. Okay? I came from a fairly messed-up family. But I got over it. I had a father who drank very heavily. It was a very dysfunctional family. My mother didn't do anything about it. She just let him walk all over her and all over us. And I decided, when I left home, that I was going to leave all that behind me.

Dr. McKay: Todd, is this new information for you, about Jacklyn's past?

Todd: I already know about her father. Jacklyn told me about him when we first met.

Dr. McKay: So sometimes she does talk a little bit and tell you some things.

Todd: She was more open in the beginning.

Dr. McKay: So in those days it seemed like you were able to learn more about her, and she was a little bit more willing to share. Jacklyn, I'm wondering if there are some other things that it would be very hard for you if Todd knew about.

Jacklyn: God, you don't give up, do you? There's some stuff. There's some stuff. There was an incident.

Dr. McKay: Uh-huh.

Jacklyn: I was ten. My father had some friends over. They were all drinking. And he had this one friend who . . . He was the CEO of a company, a very charming man. He told wonderful stories. We all loved him. I had said goodnight to everybody and was in bed. And then my bedroom door opened. He was standing there. He said, "Oh, Jackie! I forgot to give you a kiss goodnight." Then he closed the door behind him. Do I really have to talk about this?

Dr. McKay: I know this is very hard to talk about. I'm curious about what you think might happen if Todd hears this story. If he learns about what happened with that man. What do you think Todd might think? How would he feel or react to you?

Jacklyn: It's not pretty stuff. It's just . . . It's really ugly. Why should Todd see that? Why should he know about that?

Dr. McKay: But if he did see it, if he did learn about it, as he is starting to learn now, what do you think his reaction would be?

Jacklyn: I don't know. It's not like it really makes me more attractive!

Dr. McKay: You think he might think you're less attractive?

Jacklyn: Yes! Anyone who is so . . . screwed up.

Dr. McKay: He might think you're screwed up.

Jacklyn: It's a screwed-up thing. Okay? It's a screwed-up thing when a ten-year-old girl is violated.

Dr. McKay: Yes, it is screwed up. It's a terribly screwed-up thing. But I'm wondering, do you think Todd would see *you* as screwed up? That there was something wrong with you and pull away?

Jacklyn: There must have been something wrong with me, right? I was the one he did it to!

Jacklyn is starting to share things about her experience. The first thing she shares, her father's alcoholism, is something Todd already knows. She's hoping that she can end this process simply and easily by offering this tidbit. It doesn't work, because it's something that's already been shared. But now Jacklyn takes a risk. She brings up something that's painful, scary. Her strong emotions at this point create a door, an opportunity to find out what Jacklyn thinks Todd will feel and how Todd will react when he learns about this part of her experience.

Therapists call this behavioral testing—*an experiment in which the therapist leads you through a scenario, causing you to take a risk—breaking an internal rule about not ever saying anything about the shameful, scary, painful parts of your experience. And then what happens when you do? Are you rejected? Is your partner turned off? Does your partner turn away? Or does that revelation and that willingness to be open actually increase the closeness and intimacy in the relationship? Right now we're finding out. We're learning more about it. We started out by learning what Jacklyn's assumptions were. Next we will turn to Todd and find out what his reactions to Jacklyn's revelations will be.*

Dr. McKay: So you think that Todd would pull away if he knows about this. Let me ask Todd. As you're listening to this experience— we don't know everything about it, we don't know everything that happened—but as you're listening to this experience, what's your reaction? What happens inside of you?

Todd: God, my heart just goes out to her! Jacklyn, I had no idea! How hideous for you! It just makes me want to hold you and comfort you. It makes me want to punch that guy's lights out.

Dr. McKay: So you're angry at the man, and you're concerned for Jacklyn.

Todd: Yeah.

Dr. McKay: Jacklyn, is that what you expected, or does that feel different from what you expected? You took a big risk.

Jacklyn: It wasn't something I was planning on talking about. I guess I thought it was a little too disgusting to talk about, to tell Todd. It's not something I'm proud of.

Dr. McKay: But what are you hearing from Todd?

Jacklyn: He sounds very supportive of me. Very protective of me. It's nice to hear.

Dr. McKay: It's a little bit of a surprise, huh?

Jacklyn: This kind of thing hasn't been a big part of our relationship. Like you say, it's been kind of a good-time relationship. I didn't expect we'd have to go through something like this together.

Dr. McKay: And your prediction was that Todd would push you away if you did. But instead, what's happening is that Todd is—psychologically, emotionally—putting his arms around you and wanting to be there for you as you experience these feelings and share this memory. Are you getting that, too?

Jacklyn: I'm hearing him say that. And I believe him, because Todd's a really sincere person.

Jacklyn is struggling with something psychologists call shame-based relating. *Shame-based relating grows from a perception of the self as flawed, bad, wrong. This sense is not so much based on events but on feelings. The person sees him- or herself as someone whose core experience—what it is to be alive, aware, conscious—is not okay, is not acceptable. In his or her attempts to hide, the person constructs an entire, attractive persona that will allow competent relating, allowing him or her to belong, to be part of a group. This persona will also protect the individual from being exposed, from having all those unacceptable parts brought to light, and from experiencing the humiliation of having those parts seen and known. The task of the therapy dialogue, where commitment struggles are based on shame, is first to uncover these core beliefs and then to recognize them as the poisonous falsehoods they are—wrong-headed, misguiding lies that can and should be rejected.*

Jacklyn, Todd, and I continued this dialogue over the course of two more therapy sessions through the dark forest of Jacklyn's beliefs until we arrived at a place from which the view was suddenly clear.

Dr. McKay: You know, Jacklyn, I think something very important happened a few weeks ago, when you shared a memory that ordinarily wouldn't feel very comfortable, very safe to share. There was a part of you that said, "If I share this, Todd is going to pull away. He's going to see there's something wrong with me." And, in a way, that was an experiment. It was an opportunity to examine the fear that if you expose some part of yourself that ordinarily you would keep hidden, something bad will happen. But it didn't turn out that way. And I'm wondering, Jacklyn, if there are some other things that are really scary or difficult to talk to Todd about, to share with him, about what it feels like to be you. Not just events, not just things that have happened. But what it really feels like to be you, to be the person Jacklyn.

Jacklyn: Is that something anyone can ever really understand? I mean, what it's like to be inside someone else's skin, inside his or her mind? Is that something people *should* share? I don't think I'd want Todd to know what it feels like to be me.

Dr. McKay: You're not sure that's something it makes sense to share. What happens if you don't share it, Jacklyn? Let me ask you that. What's going to happen to you in this relationship and in your life if you aren't able to share what it feels like to be you?

Jacklyn: I guess you probably want me to say I'll feel isolated— socially isolated, emotionally isolated. Is that the right answer?

Dr. McKay: I don't know. I guess what I'm wondering is what *your* answer is.

Jacklyn: I don't know that it's necessarily my goal to just tear my chest open and have people look in.

Dr. McKay: That's not what I asked you. I understand that you don't want to expose your most private feelings to the whole world. But I'm asking what's going to happen in this relationship and in future relationships if you have any? What's going to happen if you keep those things to yourself, if your partner never knows what it feels like to be Jacklyn?

Jacklyn: I'll be safe.

Dr. McKay: You'll be safe. That's right. That's one thing that'll happen. You'll feel safe, and you will not have to deal with the feelings of shame that would result from those things being seen and known. That's right. Anything else?

Jacklyn: Well, Todd's kind of threatening to leave me if I don't open up some more.

Dr. McKay: So you might lose those relationships, your relationship with Todd or some other relationship. After a while, those relationships might slip away.

Jacklyn: I guess you want to show as much as you need to show to keep a relationship that you want to keep, but hold back what you need to hold back to feel safe.

Dr. McKay: It's a hard balance, isn't it?

Jacklyn: Yeah.

Dr. McKay: Todd, what do you think? Is the balance working?

Todd: No, it's not working for me! I mean, it's too much on the side of safety and not enough on the side of sharing and being close.

We're like a plane that has all its cargo on the port side, and we're flying uneven, crooked in the sky. That doesn't feel good to me!

Dr. McKay: So it's really out of balance for you.

Todd: Way out of balance.

Dr. McKay: So, Jacklyn, one of the things that could happen is that relationships get out of balance and your partner doesn't feel close enough to really feel connected, to really feel intimate.

Jacklyn: Yeah. Well, I'm willing to try to be closer and share more. I guess.

Dr. McKay: Would you be willing to try another little experiment today like the one that we did a few weeks ago?

Jacklyn: I guess. Yeah.

Dr. McKay: Okay. I want to talk a little more, but not about an event or experience or what anyone did to you. But more about what it feels like to be *you*. I'm wondering if you can talk a little bit about what that feels like. You're all alone, you're by yourself . . .

Jacklyn: It feels like I need to put on my face for the world. I need to put on my best face.

Dr. McKay: Because if you don't, what would the world see? What would Todd see?

Jacklyn: He wouldn't want to see it. I wouldn't want him to see it!

Dr. McKay: What would Todd see if you didn't put on your face? What feelings would he see?

Jacklyn: He'd see someone who shouldn't be looked at by anybody, who shouldn't even be in a room with mirrors . . . Somebody really hideous.

Dr. McKay: So that's a scary thing, to think that he would see something that he would think is hideous. And that's the voice inside you, the shame voice that says, "If he ever knew any of these things, boy, he'd run for the hills! He'd think you're ugly and run away." And what is it like then, this thing that's so hard to talk about? I appreciate that this is hard. What is it like to be you? What are those feelings that you're afraid Todd wouldn't want to see?

Jacklyn: You're so empathic, you should be able to tell. You should be able to know! You want to know? Do you want me to tell you what it's like? Well, here's Jacklyn! Here's Jacklyn in her evening gown, at the cocktail party, looking gorgeous. You know what she looks like inside? Like a monster! You see that woman with the slim figure? You should see her two hours after the party in front of a half-gallon of ice cream, just eating the entire thing. Eating it all down. That person at the party isn't really me. The person who's really me is the person eating that half-gallon of ice cream one spoonful at a time, and then maybe going on to another half-gallon of ice cream! You'd see the person who gets so full with the food that she doesn't have to think anymore. She *can't* think anymore. It's the only way to shut up that voice inside me, the voice that goes over every single thing that was said at the party, every single stupid thing I said, every faux pas. Everything my client said that wasn't right. It all reflects on me! It's a mirror that shows that most hideous self, the ugliest self, the stupidest self, the piece-of-shit self. Okay? Are you satisfied? Look at me! I've cried off all my makeup. I hate you!

Dr. McKay: I know it's hard. This is the hardest thing in the world, to open this part of yourself.

Jacklyn: Now you see the real Jacklyn. Look at me!

Dr. McKay: And what do you think Todd will feel?

Jacklyn: (*crying*) I hate it that he's seeing me like this! I hate it! I want to hide.

Dr. McKay: Yes. But what do you think he sees? And what do you think he feels as he looks at your pain?

Jacklyn: He sees a hideously flawed woman, someone who is all surface. And when you crack that surface, underneath there's this ugliness.

Dr. McKay: I hear you. That's what you think. And that's why you haven't shared it with him. That's why you haven't opened those parts of yourself. I understand.

Jacklyn: Well, the cat's out of the bag, isn't it?

Dr. McKay: But the hiding left you very alone, didn't it? You've been very alone. You had to live behind that person you created for everyone to look at; for Todd to look at.

Jacklyn: But now I don't even have that barrier anymore!

Dr. McKay: I understand. Let me turn to Todd for a minute. I want you to listen carefully to what happens now. Todd, I want to ask you a question. Jacklyn has shared some incredibly hard-to-express feelings. And I'm wondering what's happening inside of you as you listen.

Todd: I feel grateful! Jacklyn, I never saw this part of you before. To me, you're beautiful!

Dr. McKay: When you say "beautiful," what's the beauty that you see?

Todd: Well, her vulnerability. She's never shown me that before. She's always been so strong about everything, and it makes me just want to put my arms around her. I don't know. It makes me feel like maybe she does need me. Maybe I am, or can be, someone important to her.

Dr. McKay: There's something you have to give her. What do you have to give Jacklyn in terms of these feelings she's shared with you?

Todd: Acceptance, I guess. Acceptance and love. I just need to listen!

Dr. McKay: Jacklyn, how does what Todd is saying about his feelings compare to what you thought he would say, what that voice inside you expected him to say, predicted he would say?

Jacklyn: It's different.

Dr. McKay: How so?

Jacklyn: I never wanted him to see this part of me! And I didn't expect him to react like this. I'm touched. It makes me feel loved.

Dr. McKay: So the voice says, "He'll resist this. He'll resent this. He'll push away. He'll think you're ugly." But we're hearing something very different. And this is a surprise. Why, do you think, is Todd's reaction so different from what the voice says?

Jacklyn: I don't know.

Dr. McKay: Your voice might not be telling you the truth, huh?

Jacklyn: I guess not.

Jacklyn's revelation about her binging led to a referral for individual therapy aimed at changing her behavior. Eating disorders can be serious and even life threatening. People exhibiting these symptoms need professional help to change their relationship with food.

Dr. McKay: Jacklyn, I want you to keep in mind that two very important things have happened in our therapy so far. You've shared with Todd about what happened with that business associate of your father's and the way he violated you. A terrible experience. But Todd didn't react the way the voice said. Todd had a very different experience. And now when you share with him what it feels like to come back from a party and to feel those voices tearing at you, criticizing you, ripping you apart, and then to try to eat them away, Todd's reaction is again very different. Instead of Todd thinking that you are disgusting and bad and you should be ashamed, his reaction is to feel that he's finally being let in, that he's finally being allowed to be part of your inner life. And to be grateful for that, to feel more love. Such a surprise.

Jacklyn: It's shown me a part of Todd I didn't know was there. I guess I never gave him the chance to show me.

Dr. McKay: You never gave him the chance. Now let me go back to Todd for a minute. When we first started talking, you had a theory about what was going on in this relationship. Jacklyn seemed to be resisting living together. She didn't want to share a whole lot. She often didn't talk and wasn't close to you in the ways that you wanted her to be. Your theory was that maybe she just regarded you as somebody to have fun with, but not really worthy of a commitment. I'm wondering what you think now, if that theory has changed in any way.

Todd: Yeah. It seems that it really didn't have that much to do with me. It had to do with Jacklyn's feelings about herself. I guess maybe that was something in *my* head. Maybe I sometimes felt like I wasn't in her league. But I've gotta say that right now I feel more like I'm sitting in her part of the plane.

Dr. McKay: It's better balanced.

Todd: Yeah.

Dr. McKay: Jacklyn, you've worked very, very hard over the years at not having to feel shame. Not having to be exposed, having those feelings and that pain out there where someone could see them. And you've done a good job. But it's been so costly, because it's meant being alone in some ways, being emotionally cut off. Relationships can only grow to a certain level. Beyond that, you always put the brakes on. And I'm wondering what you think might happen if you and Todd continue to share more with each other.

Jacklyn: *(crying)* I'd like that. I like that feeling that maybe the person I am inside can be loved, not just the person I am to the world.

Dr. McKay: Not just your public self, but who you are inside. That's a really important statement. You'd like to feel that who you are inside can be loved.

Therapist's Overview

The fear of shame is a major source of ambivalence in relationships. Some people carry a deep sense of being wrong or bad, and their life goals are (1) to avoid feeling the burn of humiliation and (2) to keep others from seeing how flawed and unworthy they are.

Vulnerability to shame can have more than one emotional root. One type of source is a *traumatic childhood event*. Experiences of abuse, neglect, or family meltdown can leave identity scar tissue. Many survivors of trauma move through the world with a feeling that they are at fault for what happened. They blame themselves with a logic that goes like this: "If I weren't bad, these bad things would never have occurred," or, "These bad things made me bad." When Jacklyn, for example, talks about her experience of sexual abuse, it's clear the abuse has made her feel there's something wrong with her.

Another source of shame is *unworthiness schemas*. Schemas are deeply held beliefs about oneself, usually formed in childhood. They are the accumulation of literally thousands of messages from parents and other family members, such as, "That was stupid." "You're self-ish." "Another first-class screwup." "Get off your lazy ass." Any one of these messages could be shrugged off easily, but taken together they can cause a broken or shaky foundation for self-esteem. In adult relationships, the unworthiness schema makes us want to hide. We work hard to keep our shameful flaws out of sight.

A third source of shame is *runaway moods*. Some people have such strong emotions that they fear the humiliation of any of these overwhelming reactions being seen by others. Deep feelings of empti-ness or depression, phobias or panic, or sudden bursts of rage can all be hidden sources of shame. So we keep our distance, even in the most intimate relationships, for fear that our dark, difficult moods will be recognized. Jacklyn's struggle with self-hate is something she's determined to hide from Todd, even if it means keeping the rela-tionship on ice.

Addictions and *compulsions* are also a fertile field for shame. The problem may be substance abuse, gambling, compulsive sexual behav-ior, binging, cutting, or any habitual response that feels out of con-trol. Jacklyn was getting short-term relief from the shame, fear, and depression produced by her attacking inner voice. She could "stuff away" the feelings for a few hours. But the relief was short-lived, and the shame and self-loathing would soon return with a vengeance.

All addictions provide short-term relief from psychological pain but can produce long-term emotional and lifestyle catastrophes. Compulsive behavior can make us feel as if we've crossed over a line into unacceptability. We are messed-up people. We no longer belong in the ranks of normal, everyday folks. Once again, the result is to hide, to keep, as best we can, the shameful secret under wraps. When Jacklyn finally admitted to binging, she felt exposed and ashamed. This was the last thing she ever wanted Todd to know.

How does a person cope with deep feelings of shame? Most of us take evasive action—we build a persona or false self. The persona is a seamless, good-looking façade that we construct to show the world. The persona appears confident, even fearless. It doesn't make mistakes. The persona is smart and capable, handling everything from complicated work tasks to ordering the right wine in a restaurant. For men, the false self is often a shell of hyperconfidence—someone who knows everything and fears nothing. For women, the persona may have a hardened, tough-gal quality, in the manner of the roles so often performed on the screen by Lauren Bacall; or it may simply take the form of being cool and quiet. However the persona is constructed, its function is the same: to keep the world from knowing about the pain and struggle inside.

Personas, while helping to protect us from shame, are built at a heavy price. For one thing, they're a lot of work. It takes constant effort to keep the walls up. It feels like we are living on stage, but the performance never ends, and we can never take off the greasepaint and just be ourselves. The biggest cost is loneliness. We can't get too close for fear our flaws might show—for fear we'll be unmasked as bad and unworthy.

If our façade is penetrated, if someone catches a glimpse of us, we feel exposed, emotionally naked. We want to run if that happens. We want to keep those waves of shame from pounding us against the rocks. Jacklyn runs by staying busy, resisting any talk about her feelings, and keeping Todd at arm's length. And if she gets really scared, she may blow up the relationship and start over.

Vanquishing Shame

The fear of shame can be overcome. The need for a seamless persona can diminish. What works is to take small, incremental steps toward emotional disclosure. This is hard work, involving intensive risk taking, but the result can be deeper intimacy and stronger commitment in a relationship.

One of the best ways to confront the fear of shame is to take an honest look at your real self versus how you want to be seen. You and your partner should independently complete the following exercise and then share your answers. If your partner won't participate in the exercise, fill out the form a second time with the answers you think he or she would give. In other words, write down how you think your partner wants to be seen, as well as your take on his or her authentic self-image.

Ideal Versus Real Exercise

	How I want to be seen	How I really am
How I work	_____	_____
How I play	_____	_____
How I express myself	_____	_____
How I deal with problems	_____	_____
How I relate to friends	_____	_____
How I relate to family	_____	_____

How I relate sexually   _____   _____

How I handle responsibilities _____   _____

How I take care of myself   _____   _____

How I handle pain   _____   _____

Here's how one of my clients, a thirty-six-year-old stock analyst, completed this exercise:

Ideal Versus Real Exercise

	How I want to be seen	**How I really am**
How I work	*Competent and reliable*	*Unsure of my abilities; lazy*
How I play	*Good-time guy; fun*	*I think those are true*
How I express myself	*Articulate, compelling*	*Same*
How I deal with problems	*Able to deal with stuff*	*I drink too much*
How I relate to friends	*A good, reliable friend*	*Sometimes contemptuous*
How I relate to family	*A good son and sibling*	*I do a lot out of guilt*

	How I want to be seen	How I really am
How I relate sexually	*Open, happy, lusty*	*Needy, sometimes lonely*
How I handle responsibilities	*Reliably*	*Reliably*
How I take care of myself	*Everything's under control*	*I drink too much*
How I handle pain	*Like a man*	*Like a baby*

If you and your partner do the exercise together and are honest and open with each other, you're both going to learn a lot—not just about the images you consciously try to project but also about how you really view yourselves. Talking about the exercise can be a big step toward overcoming the fear of openness and being known. You should also talk about what it felt like to take this risk and the ways in which your partner's response to your revelations may have differed from your expectations.

Couple Interview

The following ten items provide opportunities to share important parts of your experience with your partner. Select no more than two or three to discuss at any particular time. Take turns sharing your responses to each item and talk to each other about what you've both learned. You can repeat the exercise with different (or the same) items any time you want to deepen feelings of closeness between you.

If your partner is unwilling or not ready to do the couple interview, fill in the answers you think your partner would give to each item. You can't know exactly what it's like to be inside your partner's head. However, doing the exercise in this way may greatly increase your empathy for, and understanding of, your partner's interior world, even if the picture you form is not accurate in every detail.

1. Something I'm afraid for you to know.
2. Something I'm not good at that I pretend to be.
3. The feeling that's hardest for me to control.
4. A problem I'm afraid to share.
5. What I wish I could give that I don't know how.
6. Something as a child that made me feel bad about myself.
7. Something I want that's hard to admit.
8. Something I don't like to remember from my past.
9. A feeling I'm afraid to show.
10. What hurts me most in our relationship.

Shame is one of the trickiest fears to expose because exposure is the very thing a shame-based person fears the most. It's important to approach this with great patience, care, and sensitivity. It may also be a really good idea to get the support and insight of a competent professional while you and your partner are going through this process.

You should also understand that, for some individuals, the prospect of his or her feelings being exposed may feel life threatening. Don't fool yourself into thinking that because you're ready to look inside your partner with love and acceptance, he or she is also ready to be looked at and loved. This may or may not be the case. If it's not, you should feel prepared either to live with a very closed-off person or to leave this relationship behind you. Chapter 11 gives explicit guidelines about when to keep working on a relationship and when to let go.

4

———◆———

The Emptiness Trap

If I Keep Moving, I Won't Have to Look Inside

Guy and Danielle met one summer on a wilderness expedition in Idaho. Danielle was assigned as a nurse to the group Guy was leading. In her late twenties and without much seniority at the hospital where she worked, Danielle used her nursing degree as a way of taking working vacations she wouldn't have been able to afford as a tourist.

Guy was a refreshing change from the mostly stuck-up doctors in the emergency room at the hospital where Danielle worked. Charming and boyish, he took joy in sharing his enthusiasm for the great outdoors; and, unlike the doctors, he didn't seem to expect or want anyone else to do his dirty work for him. He and Danielle were soon sharing a tent.

Once back in their real lives, Danielle began to see all sorts of things about Guy she didn't like. The unbridled enthusiasm that seemed so appealing out in the woods came across more as unfocused frenzy in the big city. He was one of the most generous people Danielle had ever met, but he was also one of the most irresponsible. The words "budget," "savings," and even "bank account" had no meaning for him at all. Coasting from one freelance job to the next, he carried a roll of cash in his pocket and happily spent it until it was gone.

Guy spent his passions in the same way, each month becoming obsessed with a new and, more often than not, extremely expensive hobby. In September it was woodworking. He took all the money he'd made over the summer and bought a top-of-the-line table saw from Italy. He spent all his free time making drawings of the million-dollar catamaran he planned to build and sail to Costa Rica. By Christmas, the saw was gathering dust in Guy's garage. In February, he bought an old MG he planned to fix up. By the time spring rolled around, the MG was composting in Danielle's driveway, much to the annoyance of her neighbors.

Guy sandwiched supermacho forays into extreme sports in between his other passions. Whether it was snowboarding or skate-boarding, depending on the season, Guy was always up for a new challenge. Danielle would tell him when he went off to a competition, "I'll see you in the emergency room!"

Guy more or less lived with Danielle, although he still paid a third of the rent on an apartment he shared with two guys in the city. He was there so seldom that they routinely used his empty room for out-of-town visitors.

Danielle loved Guy for all the same reasons that he drove her crazy. She loved his generosity and spontaneity, but the combination of these qualities often left him broke and dependent on Danielle's salary. He took them on the most amazing vacations whenever he had money and Danielle was able to get away, but anything resembling day-to-day domestic expectations instantly put Guy into a bad mood. Danielle loved that he was different from the dour, busi-nesslike doctors she worked with, but she also wished that Guy would just get it together and grow up.

She wanted to be able to depend on Guy—to know that he'd come up with his part of the rent every month and, maybe later on, his part of the mortgage. She needed to know that decisions they made together, like buying a house or having a child, wouldn't just go the way of Guy's other short-lived enthusiasms.

Guy told her he loved her, and he really did seem to love her. The problem wasn't a lack of feelings for Danielle, or even a lack of faith-fulness. The problem seemed to be with the very idea of commit-ment itself—not just to a relationship, but to anything at all.

Guy and Danielle's Commitment Dialogue

Danielle: We've more or less been living together. But I want to know where this is going. He's gotta make the commitment.

Dr. McKay: And what's happening right now in your relationship that makes this important to resolve?

Danielle: I mean, where is he? He's got his life with me. In reality, he's staying at my house 360 days out of the year—

Guy: Except when I'm traveling.

Danielle: Yeah, well, math never was my strong point. You know what I mean. He's got this other apartment that he still pays for. I mean, it's not cheap to pay one-third of the rent for an apartment in San Francisco. But the money's only part of it. It's like he has another life—that apartment and those friends—that he's keeping in reserve for himself.

Dr. McKay: That he's not ready to give up.

Danielle: Yeah. And then there's all the other stuff—his wilderness adventures . . . There's just so much going on. First it's one thing that's the most important thing in the world for him, and he's completely obsessed with it, and then it's something else. I don't have a sense that he's able to focus on us, on this relationship, and what's going to happen with us. I want to know what's going to happen with us! You know, I'm not getting any younger! I'm at a point where I want to start getting serious about things.

Dr. McKay: Guy, on your end, what do you want in your relationship to Danielle? What kind of relationship do you see in the future?

Guy: I've got to admit that I'm not someone who likes thinking about the future a lot. My whole thing is the present moment. And the present is exciting. It's rich. It's challenging. It gets my adrenalin going. This is what excites me. This is what I want. And Danielle is part of that!

Dr. McKay: So you have a lot of things happening. You've got those wilderness excursions you lead, and you have friends you hang out with. You're interested in sports. And Danielle is exciting, and you enjoy being with her; but you're saying that there's a lot going on in your life. And you don't think about the future. You're just enjoying the present.

Guy: That's right. *Right now* is the only thing that can matter. We don't know what's going to happen, and I don't think it makes any sense to live for a future that we don't know about, that we can't define.

Dr. McKay: Guy, let me ask you this. When you think about the future that Danielle has in mind, what does that feel like?

Guy: It feels too small to me. I have this sense of doors closing, like I'm walking down a corridor and, as I'm walking, all these doors are closing.

Dr. McKay: The doors of possibility?

Guy: Yes. And I want to know what's behind all those doors. Maybe behind one of them is something that I've always wanted, or something that's really going to change my life in an important way, or make me feel more passionate about something than I've ever felt before. I feel like all these doors are closing if I step into this one future, step into this movie she's making about "our" future.

Dr. McKay: And what does it feel like when those doors of possibility close, when you're walking down that hall and you can't open those doors and look to see what's behind them?

Guy: It feels awful.

Dr. McKay: Awful in what way?

Guy: I feel a sense of loss.

Dr. McKay: And your life with Danielle? What does that feel like if those doors are closed?

Guy: Well, it's good and everything. It's a really good thing we've got. But by itself . . . I don't know if it's enough.

Dr. McKay: Not enough?

Guy: I don't know! Maybe it is enough, but I don't know. And how can I know it's enough unless I know what else is out there?

Dr. McKay: And maybe something else would come along that would be *more*, that would give you more of something that you need.

Guy: I remember reading something in college—I think it was one of the Greek philosophers. His idea was that we all started out in the world as these creatures that had two heads and four arms and four legs, and we kind of cartwheeled around the world. But then at some point the gods separated us into creatures with just one head and just two arms and two legs. And so we're sort of doomed to go through life looking for the half we lost.

Dr. McKay: So you feel like our job is to look for our other half. And if we can't stay free to find that person, what happens to us?

Guy: What would happen? I love Danielle, I really do. But what would happen if I found this person who was my soul mate? I don't know if Danielle is that lost other half. I mean, maybe she is, but I don't know.

Dr. McKay: So you might feel a tremendous sense of deprivation if you later found that other half and couldn't have that. Perhaps you would . . . what? You would want to leave Danielle?

Guy: It's just that we can't know.

Danielle: You know, Guy, I am not at all comfortable with the idea of being in this relationship with you when you're waiting for Miss Other Half to walk in the door! I mean, for God's sake! Here we are, either we're in this relationship together or we're not. I don't know if I'm your lost half, but I'm *me*, and I thought you loved me. I know

I've loved you. But, you know what? I'm getting really sick of this. I'm getting really tired of it. It's like you want everything.

Dr. McKay: I want to just interrupt you for a second, Danielle, because what you're saying is important. You want to be in a relationship with someone who really believes you are "the one," that you are the most important, you are the person they want to spend their life with. But I think there's something going on here with Guy that we need to pay attention to and dig a little deeper to understand. I want to get back to what you're saying. But I think I want to do that after we've reached a better understanding about what really lies beneath Guy's concern about whether you're his other half. Is that okay with you?

Danielle: I guess so. Sure.

Dr. McKay: Thanks. Guy, let me ask you a question. That feeling of the doors closing, of the possibilities being shut off, of the possibility of your other half being out there somewhere but you're not allowed to look for her. And if she should show up in your life, you're not allowed to reach out to her and take her in your arms. That feeling—what is that feeling like for you? What is it like to live with those doors of possibility shut?

Guy: I wouldn't allow it. It would be too hard.

Dr. McKay: Try to imagine it, though.

Guy: It's painful.

Dr. McKay: What kind of pain is that?

Guy: It's a pain I'm not even willing to tolerate. Why should I? If Danielle loves me, why would she make me?

Dr. McKay: But I think you know about that pain. I think maybe you've lived with it for years. This pain has been part of your life for a long, long time. And periodically it shows up and has tremendous power to disturb and hurt you. Tell me about some times when that pain has showed up in your life.

Guy: I'm sorry, you've lost me. I'm not sure what you're talking about.

Dr. McKay: Remember we were talking about this feeling of the doors closing, the possibilities shutting down . . .

Guy: It was just like a metaphor.

Dr. McKay: Yeah, it is a metaphor. But the feeling you described is a very real feeling, and it's a feeling I think you're very familiar with. Wouldn't you say that it's a feeling you've known from other periods of your life?

Guy: I guess I don't understand what makes you say that.

Dr. McKay: What makes me say it is your absolute certainty that you don't want to live with it. You're telling us today that this is something you will not do, you will not live with in your life. It sounds like something you're familiar with, and it's something that has been profoundly painful to you.

Guy: If it is something I've been experiencing, it's not a place where I've stayed very long. You know, it's like touching something hot—you pull your hand away.

Dr. McKay: You try to get away from it as soon as possible. But it burns like hell.

Guy: It burns like hell. You know it's going to burn like hell, and you take your hand away. Because, you know, only an idiot would keep their hand on that.

Dr. McKay: And you know one of the things that can put your hand on that hot place is to feel closed in. And you've been in that place. You've experienced that feeling.

Guy: To tell you the truth, all these things they make you do when you're growing up—I hated that. I was always resistant to the idea of having to go down one straight and narrow path. Having to choose one profession and be one kind of guy and marry one woman. The possibilities are so wide, and it seems our choices are so narrow!

Dr. McKay: You like to keep a lot of options. That's why you're designing the catamaran and thinking about restoring that MG and leading the wilderness tours in the summer. You've got a lot of things you do.

Guy: And Danielle—she's part of that.

Dr. McKay: And Danielle's part of it.

Danielle: Oh, can I wake up now?

Dr. McKay: Just a minute, Danielle. Because, Guy, if you didn't have those things—all that intense activity, that involvement, that excitement—what would happen?

Danielle: He should come with me into the emergency room if he wants excitement. He'd get so much excitement that he'd just be longing to be in a place where things were stable. Where people weren't dying every second or threatening to die on you every second. Believe me!

Dr. McKay: So you're not sure you understand what Guy's talking about—what this excitement is that he needs.

Danielle: It sounds nuts to me! It just sounds nuts.

Dr. McKay: And yet it's something that's having a big impact on your relationship. It's hard to understand, and yet it's an unseen force that lies behind Guy's decision to keep the apartment in San Francisco, even though he lives there only a few nights out of the year.

Danielle: I want to hear it. I want to hear what you come up with here.

Dr. McKay: Well, we're going to learn a little more. Guy, I know this is hard to look at, and you talked about it being like a burning experience that can sear and hurt you. And yet I think that we need to spend enough time trying to retrieve what that experience is like, so we can understand how it's influencing your decisions today with Danielle. Can you go back to a time when you were aware of the doors of possibility closing, the excitement dying—a kind of lack of connection, involvement, intensity? Can you remember a time like that?

Guy: Yeah, I can. I remember the day after I graduated from college, and I knew I was suddenly expected to be this grown-up who's just going to do one thing, one boring thing from now on.

Dr. McKay: Boring. What does it mean to be bored in that sense? Just the same thing over and over again. What is that feeling like?

Guy: It's like there's no protection, no cushion.

Dr. McKay: There's no cushion between you and what?

Guy: I guess it's like this sense of nothingness, like it all boils down to nothing. There's nothing there.

Dr. McKay: Is it an empty feeling?

Guy: Yeah. I don't mean anything, my life doesn't mean anything, nothing has meaning. It's this kind of . . . hunger.

Dr. McKay: So it's a need for intensity, meaning, connection, excitement that pushes boredom and emptiness away.

Guy: Well, feeling like maybe there's a possibility of filling the emptiness, of escaping that sense of, that fear of meaninglessness.

Dr. McKay: Are you afraid of feeling empty with Danielle? Of someday being in a place where you're feeling empty and bored and stuck?

Guy: That's what happens, isn't it? You settle down with one person—I know all these people, all these friends of my parents and my parents, too. They all started out in love. They fall in love, get married, and have some kids. And sooner or later, they're just bored with their lives. They give up!

Dr. McKay: And that feeling is a very painful feeling. It sounds like it's a depressing, disconnected, meaningless, empty life.

Guy: It's like death, like a living death.

Dr. McKay: That's a very scary thing, seeing people who were once in love lose their passion for each other. And that's what you're afraid will happen with you and Danielle.

Guy: I've seen it happen so many times. I don't want it to happen with us . . . But I don't want to lose her either.

Danielle: You know what? In my work I meet a lot of people, and there are people who think I'm attractive. I love you, Guy. But you've got to figure out what you want. I'm tired of waiting.

Dr. McKay: And for you, Guy, the fear is, if you make a commitment to Danielle, and these doors of possibility close, then you're going to be vulnerable to the feelings of emptiness, meaninglessness, depression, and boredom.

Guy: Well, that's not happening now. You know, my life is good. It's full of excitement. Full of lots of stuff, including Danielle.

We've reached a point in the therapy dialogue where Guy needs to be prodded toward a recognition that he's being paralyzed by his fear.

Dr. McKay: And now what's happened is a crisis, because Danielle is saying you've got to make up your mind. There's a choice here, and it's a very difficult choice. The choice is between a commitment that risks your feeling that emptiness versus losing Danielle. It's a tough one.

Guy: I hate these choices! It's like you've got to make your life smaller. It's shrinking your horizons. I thought the idea was that, in relationships, you broaden your horizons. You make your lives bigger, not smaller.

Dr. McKay: And it feels like Danielle is asking you to shrink your life. Now, let me ask you a really important question, Guy. When that feeling of emptiness comes up, that feeling we've been talking about—the bored, disconnected feeling that's so painful—how long does it usually last?

This is a key question, because people who struggle with emptiness often regard it as a monolith—something that will overtake them and crush them, something that will never stop, never remit. In fact, emptiness is just a temporary state. It's like a wave. Very often the feeling of emptiness, depression, or disconnection may last no more than a few hours or a few days. But the person who fears emptiness thinks of it as eternal, as something that must be avoided at all costs, because once it catches up with them, they will sink beneath it and drown.

Guy: I've never stayed there long enough to find out.

Dr. McKay: But you have been there at times. How long does it usually last?

Guy: I don't know . . .

Dr. McKay: Ten minutes? A few hours?

Guy: No. It's more like . . . Well, I guess it's gone on for days before.

Dr. McKay: Sometimes it's gone on for some days?

Guy: Yeah. Maybe even weeks.

Dr. McKay: So there have been times when you've felt it for a while.

Guy: I think the last time I felt it was right before we took this great trip.

Dr. McKay: You and Danielle?

Guy: Yeah, we went to France. We rented these motorbikes, and we went to the Grand Prix. We had an incredible time. We dressed up. It was wild. And, you know, that feeling was gone as soon as we got on that plane and left. It was gone.

Dr. McKay: So you were feeling empty before, but then getting on the plane and doing something intense and involving together seemed to drive it away. Have you ever had other experiences with Danielle when you had a period of emptiness?

Guy: I don't know. Danielle, can you think of any times?

Danielle: Yeah, I can think of times. I mean, I never thought of it as emptiness. I just thought you were in a shitty mood. You know, you were kind of remote and distant from me. There was that time last Christmas. You were really weird! It was an awful time for me, actually.

Dr. McKay: Do you remember that, Guy?

Guy: Yeah, I do. That's a hard time of year for me.

Dr. McKay: Was that an empty time for you?

Guy: Yeah, it was. You know, there was nothing going on. I was off work. Danielle was off work, and we were going to her family's house for the holidays and, God, it was just . . . I felt really stuck.

Dr. McKay: How long did it go on?

Guy: It lasted through the holidays. I hated it.

Dr. McKay: And how did you get out of it?

Guy: I led this incredible winter trip, a winter camping trip in Idaho.

Dr. McKay: So you had an adventure where you led one of the wilderness groups?

Guy: That snapped me out of it.

Dr. McKay: I want to talk a little bit to both of you about what it means to struggle with emptiness. This is not uncommon. A lot of people carry inside them a tendency at times to feel empty. And you're right, Guy, it helps to have intense activities—the wilderness adventures; the skateboarding and snowboarding; a strong, intense relationship with Danielle. All of these things can give you a sense of involvement and connection and excitement that keeps that emptiness at bay. But you sense that it's there somewhere, lurking. And the thing that makes commitment scary is wondering what happens if you make a life with Danielle and your worlds become interconnected and that emptiness comes roaring up. You think you're helpless, that it's going to overtake you, consume you, and there's nothing you can do.

Guy: It's like that sense of no way out—that avalanche of snow, and you're buried.

Dr. McKay: And making a commitment to the relationship, it feels like now you're stuck with the emptiness. There's no escaping it. Whereas if you don't make a commitment, it feels like there's always the possibility of finding your soul mate. There's the possibility of the other half or some other kind of relationship or some other kind of involvement that will give you a sense of intensity that will help drive the emptiness back.

Guy: That's right.

Dr. McKay: The emptiness feels like a state of emergency, something that has to be stopped at all costs; and you have to keep an open, uncommitted relationship, so you can have exit strategies—like getting into another relationship or having another sexual involvement—

Guy: Having the power to do it, the freedom to do it.

Dr. McKay: You feel like you need the freedom to do something that will help stop the emptiness. This is an emergency, and you have tools to stop it.

Guy: I need to have my entire self available.

Dr. McKay: And if you close the doors of possibility on those other relationships, on those other people, on those other sources of intensity and excitement and sexuality, maybe you'll be stuck with the emptiness and never be able to escape. But what I want to propose to you is that, instead of emptiness being a state of emergency, it is just a temporary wave. You've had it many times in your life. We've explored a couple of the times that it's come up during your relationship with Danielle, and you've found ways of pushing it away, of putting it aside. In one case you guys took a trip to France. In another case you led a winter wilderness trip. You already have skills and techniques for coping with the feeling of emptiness.

Danielle: Can I break in here for a minute? You know, this kind of hurts me—the whole idea that I'm someone he feels empty with, but that there's some other mythical person out there that he wouldn't feel empty with. Is this about some lack of feeling he has for me? Because if that's the case—

Dr. McKay: I don't think that's what Guy is saying. It's not that there's something wrong in the relationship with you; but there's the fear that should the emptiness overtake him, he'll drown in it. He'll be helpless to do anything about it.

Danielle: Well, why can't my love for him, or our feelings for each other, be something that keeps him from feeling empty?

Dr. McKay: We're going to explore how to do that. That's exactly the next step in the process we're working on. I'm glad you brought that up, because deepening the relationship you and Guy have is where we're going to find answers. Because if this relationship is going to work, we're going to have to find a way of responding to Guy's struggle with feelings of emptiness. But step one is to be able to recognize that emptiness, when it comes up, is not a state of emergency, even though it's painful and uncomfortable. It's a wave that passes. And, Guy, it's a wave that you've suffered many times and that has passed many times. We can figure out strategies inside the relationship to help you get through that wave, help it pass more quickly and with less disruption and less pain.

Guy: Why is it that I'm feeling this? Is there something wrong with me?

Dr. McKay: You know, Guy, I think a lot of us grow up with sort of a built-in, hardwired experience of being alone on some level. We yearn for connection, for intensity, for some kind of experience that will fill us up, that can keep that emptiness, that loneliness, that depressed feeling at bay. And I think many of us struggle with it our whole lives.

Guy: So it's just like a human thing? Is it a male thing?

Dr. McKay: I think it's a human thing. I think some people have more of it, and some people have less. Like some people have brown hair, and some people have blond hair. Some people are shy, and some people are outgoing. I think some people struggle more with feelings of emptiness, aloneness, and disconnection, and others are less vulnerable to them.

Danielle: Okay, fine. But my question is, what are we going to do in this relationship? Do you want it or don't you, Guy?

Dr. McKay: And we're working toward looking at one of the big obstacles to making a commitment, which is Guy's fear of being helplessly stuck with these empty feelings. They come along, and he has no answer for them. There's nothing he can do, no way of coping, and he just feels like he might go under. That's part of what's keeping him on the fence. And we're looking more deeply at that. Now let me turn to you, Guy. You know, I'm wondering, when this feeling comes up, what would it be like if you acknowledged that the empty feeling was happening and shared that with Danielle? What would it be like for you to say it out loud to her?

Guy: I've never told anybody before when it was happening. It doesn't seem like the kind of thing you talk about. But I guess now that everything's kind of out on the table more, maybe I could say something to Danielle.

Dr. McKay: You could say, "I'm feeling that feeling"?

Guy: Yeah, I think I could say that. It wasn't even something I had a name for before.

Dr. McKay: What would it be like for you, Danielle, if Guy were to say to you, "I'm having that empty feeling right now, and it's really hard"?

Danielle: I'd say, lie down here, honey. I'll take care of you. This is what I do! I'll monitor your vital signs. I'll give you the medicine you need. I'll call in the right people. And I will not leave your side.

Dr. McKay: Guy, does that seem reassuring to you, or does it seem kind of like hubris—that she really doesn't understand what this feeling is like?

Guy: You know, it kind of cracks me up. I know she's a great emergency room nurse. And if I ever were in some kind of really bad accident, Danielle's the one I would definitely want to have at my bedside.

Dr. McKay: But that empty feeling is different from an emergency. It's a wave. It comes, and it feels very uncomfortable. Then, after a while, it recedes and is gone. But while you're under the wave, it's very, very painful and sometimes very scary. I guess I'm wondering what you think it would feel like to share that with Danielle? You said you could do it. What would it feel like for her to hear and know that at that moment you were in the middle of one of those empty waves?

Guy: I guess maybe it would be like when you're a kid and you go to the beach and you get knocked down by one of those big breakers. You're under the water, and you just think, "Uh-oh, I'm gonna drown!" You just see all the mud and water swirling around, and you know you can't get any air.

Dr. McKay: Do you think she could reach in for you and pull you up?

Guy: That's what you want in that moment. You want somebody who's going to reach in for you.

Dr. McKay: Let's talk about that for a minute. Let's say one of those waves hits, for whatever reason. It might be the holidays, it might be that you haven't had enough stimulation or connection, or it's been a while since you led a wilderness trip. You're feeling a little less close to Danielle. It could be any of a million reasons, but something stimulates that wave of emptiness, and so you share with Danielle what's going on. I want to ask the two of you, what do you think that you could do together that would help with that wave? It might not end it instantly, but it would help with the wave. For Guy, there would need to be some sense of control, something that he can do or you can do together to diminish its impact.

Danielle: You know, I hate to keep going back to the emergency room. But I can imagine it's like the patient who's in a lot of pain. We know the pain is temporary, that it's going to go away. It's post-surgery, post-trauma, and we've got a drip going with pain medication. And the patient himself is able to control the amount of medication he gets to control his own pain. But I'm also there if the pain gets too bad. I'm there with a cool washcloth on his face. I'm there with fresh sheets. I'm there to make sure his vital signs are okay. So it's a team effort. It's the person suffering the pain, but I'm part of it, too. And we also know the pain is temporary; it's going to get better. I always tell them, "This, too, will pass." It seems to help.

Dr. McKay: What's going on for you, Guy, as you listen to Danielle?

Guy: Well, I don't know. I don't want to think of myself as the guy who's in all the pain, the guy who's so screwed up. But, on the other hand, I like the idea that she'd be there to help me make it better. To get through it together.

Dr. McKay: So let's look at that specifically. If you were to acknowledge to Danielle that you were feeling that kind of emptiness come up, what specifically could the two of you do together to have an effect on it?

Guy: Well, it seems like in the past when this has come up, what's solved the crisis for me is doing something exciting. And maybe we could have an agreement to do something exciting.

Dr. McKay: If you're feeling in the middle of a wave, you and Danielle would cook up something exciting to do together.

Danielle: Yeah, I'd tell him: Hey, you! Get down on that kitchen table and take off your clothes. We're going to do something exciting!

Dr. McKay: That might be one exciting thing. So knowing that the two of you were committed to creating an experience, whatever it might be—it could be a sexual experience, it could be a trip, it could be inviting a bunch of friends over for a raucous evening. But whatever it is, something that would be intense and stimulating and help with that wave. Guy, you're an expert on this. I know you've tried to stay away from the feeling and you've pushed it and kept it at bay as best you can. But you've had a lot of experience with it, some with Danielle but certainly at other times in your life. What do you think the two of you could do together? How could you and Danielle team up to get you through the emptiness?

Guy: I can imagine maybe when I'm in those places, if we could just spend some really intense time together where she'd be taking care of me for a change instead of all these other people she takes care of, and really focus on . . . It sounds funny to say, but maybe I could just be really selfish. Maybe I wouldn't be thinking about anything except my own comfort and feeling good. You know, Danielle, you and your girlfriends once in a while go off to that spa, have a spa day. Maybe this would be like Guy's spa day. You'd be taking care of me.

Dr. McKay: How do you feel about that idea, Danielle?

Danielle: Well, I can imagine it might be kind of fun in some ways. It could be. As long as he doesn't . . . I don't know . . . Are you going to want me to dress up in high-heeled boots and a bustier or something?

Dr. McKay: What do you think, Guy? What do you have in mind?

Guy: Well, I wasn't thinking of anything quite so kinky. But sex would be part of it. Maybe having it be a little freer. Having it be different. Having it for me, until I felt better.

It takes a lot of effort and dedication—even selflessness—to deal with the kind of fear that Guy has. If you choose someone like that for a partner, it's going to add a real burden to your part of the relationship—and it's not fair on some level. But, if Danielle wants to be with Guy, that's the only way it's going to work.

Dr. McKay: What else might the two of you do?

Guy: I think it would be really nice to go somewhere really beautiful and warm and just sit in the sun together, maybe on the sand, and lie there with my head on Danielle's bosom and listen to the waves.

Danielle: I can't believe you said the word "bosom"!

Dr. McKay: So be in a beautiful place, feel connected, try to find some peace there as well as have this really strong, intense sexual connection that's about giving you some healing.

Guy: Just till the wave passed.

Dr. McKay: Danielle, what's happening for you as you're listening to Guy's idea?

Danielle: To tell you the truth, all of this stuff sounds pretty nice to me. I don't mind the idea at all! I wish we had more time together like that. I mean, he's always running off somewhere. I like the idea of being closer.

Danielle is insightful enough to realize that Guy is doing something that's really hard for him: recognizing and verbalizing his fear. Because she wants to be with this man, she's willing to collaborate on helping him get through these periods of fear, as opposed to having him run away and use experiences outside their relationship to manage it.

Dr. McKay: So we're starting to make a plan. When that empty wave comes up, it's not a state of emergency that requires escape. Instead, you'll think of it as a wave you can get through, that'll pass over you. The two of you can work together collaboratively in a way that doesn't undermine or disrupt the relationship. One of your specific ideas is to go to a place that's warm, a place that has a beach, where you and Guy can focus on connecting intensely, sexually, in a way that feels good and nurturing and healing to him. A place where you might feel close and connected lying on the sand, enjoying the peace of this environment. You and Guy will work together to create a healing environment for a little while that will help both of you navigate that empty period. Is that what you're suggesting?

Danielle: You know, just as long as it's not always like that. Because I do enough nursing in my job. I don't want to be Guy's nurse. That's not what I want in a relationship. But as a once-in-a-while kind of thing, hey! I know how to do this stuff. This is what I do best.

Dr. McKay: I think right now Guy is struggling with the question of whether he can cope with his own feelings of emptiness and stay in this relationship. Before this point, the answer seemed to be no. He was afraid that the only way out of the emptiness was to keep the door open for some other possibility, some other exciting, intense relationship. Keeping that door open gave him a sense of control over the emptiness. What we're doing now is experimenting to see if, in fact, you and Guy can do things together to manage and get Guy through those waves of emptiness. If the experiment is successful, then Guy's anxiety about that empty feeling, and not having control over it, is likely to diminish. And it may be that the two of you can work together to cope with Guy's fear of emptiness. But right now, the jury's out. We have to see if this experiment leads you toward a deeper sense of commitment.

Therapist's Overview

The fear of emptiness is often a driving force behind commitment struggles. Identifying and confronting this fear can have a tremendous positive effect on long-term love relationships.

Emptiness takes two forms. Some people describe it as a hollowness, a yearning for something intense and distracting to fill the void. Others talk about a chronic numbness, a feeling of being shut down. Both forms of emptiness are associated with depression. And both often require high levels of stimulation and excitement for any relief. People who struggle with emptiness seek excitement in the form of risk and adventure, high-conflict situations, pressured jobs, and the heady drugs of sex and romance.

Emptiness has both biological and environmental roots. Some people describe a core loneliness and yearning that goes back as far as they can remember. "I was born hungry," one of my clients used to say. "I always wanted something to fill this place inside, and I could never find enough to escape this perpetually restless, seeking mode." Some families are crucibles for emptiness. Neglect can leave children feeling profoundly alone; chronic abuse can teach them to numb and shut off their feelings.

Whether emptiness is "hardwired" or a response to dysfunctional parenting, the result is the same—a feeling that at best you are one step ahead of depression. And you'd better keep running, or you'll sink into the void.

Here's how the fear of emptiness affects intimate partners. A new, intense sexual relationship feels great to someone coping with emptiness. It's manna from heaven. The honeymoon phase is full of sexual and emotional discovery. Everything is new, everything is interesting. For a time, the emptiness and depression are hidden by romantic love.

Then the relationship plateaus. There are conflicts, periods of withdrawal; the sexual energy subsides a little. And the shadow of emptiness returns. With it comes a restlessness. Commitment wavers; the relationship begins to feel like a trap. The only escape from emptiness and depression appears to lie in a new, intense involvement.

People who struggle with emptiness fear commitment for one reason: it ties them to a relationship that, over time, may protect them less and less from the inner void. And the commitment keeps them from seeking relief, temporary as it may be, in the arms of someone, or in the thrall of something, new.

Guy resists making a commitment to Danielle because he's running as fast as he can to keep ahead of the emptiness. He's afraid of stillness. Extreme sports, wilderness treks, and engaging new hobbies are all part of an effort to fill every moment with intense activity. He fears giving up his apartment to make a committed life with

Danielle because then he wouldn't be able to run anymore. Things would be simpler, less intense. There likely would be fewer activities, and there would be no new sexual relationships. A commitment to Danielle, Guy fears, would mean long-term vulnerability to the demons that chase him.

Coping with Emptiness

What can people do when they fear that emptiness will overwhelm them? Step one is to recognize that emptiness, like all painful emotional states, is temporary. It's a wave that will pass. When the void threatens, it feels like an emergency—something that has to be fixed right now. But if the person suffering these feelings waits without running, the pain will soften. The sadness and yearning will lose their sharp edges.

Step two for coping with emptiness is to acknowledge the feeling. Together, as partners, give a name to the experience. Stop allowing it to be the elephant in the corner. Encourage your partner to describe the loneliness and yearning or the numbness. People who experience these feelings need to give words to what has been chasing them, and, in doing so, they make it less scary. Your partner needs to make his or her emptiness a problem that the two of you can manage as a team.

The worst thing about emptiness is being alone with it. To prevent this, partners can collaborate on ways to face off the depression and vulnerability. They can, in step three, plan together a set of strategies to push the emptiness away.

Start by talking about things that have helped in the past. Then move on to brainstorming. Has spending time in nature ever helped? Or strenuous exercise? Have intensely romantic weekends ever relieved the feeling of emptiness inside your partner? How about a sensuous massage or a special sexual turn-on? Does it help to spend time with friends? To escape momentarily into movies or games? What about spending a long, quiet evening cooking, eating, and talking together?

Step four involves building something called "emptiness tolerance." Reducing one's vulnerability to emptiness requires a commitment to make several critical changes. The partner who fears emptiness will need to identify one or more meaningful activities that can carry them through periods of vulnerability and depression; and they would be well advised to learn the basics of meditation and mindfulness.

Meaningful activities are antidotes for emptiness because they focus attention outside the self. Whether people with these feelings invest energy in a creative project, in helping others, or in taking steps toward the achievement of an important goal, they end up feeling they've done something of value. Partners can often do these activities together, reinforcing each other's commitment to finding meaning during difficult times.

Meditation can be the most effective tool for developing emptiness tolerance. Meditation helps people move through these feelings to a place of calm and peace inside themselves. It helps them learn how to soothe their yearning while being quiet and alone. The related discipline of mindfulness helps people fill their awareness with sensations in the here and now rather than focusing on what's missing or wished for.

The Emptiness Questionnaire

Before moving on to the exercises that follow, we'd recommend that both you and your partner fill out the following questionnaire. It's called the Haight Ashbury Mood Scale (1995: Buggs, Korbana, McKay, and Rogers), and it measures the experience of emptiness. Scores below 26 suggest the presence—at least occasionally—of feelings and fears of emptiness. You and your partner may both find the results enlightening and a helpful starting point for a discussion about the role of emptiness in your partner's life. If your partner does not choose to fill out the questionnaire, then you might jump straight to the action plans.

Haight Ashbury Mood Scale

Instructions: Use the following scale to describe your present feelings as you respond to the statements below:

1—ALWAYS	4—OCCASIONALLY	6—ALMOST NEVER
2—ALMOST ALWAYS	5—RARELY	7—NEVER
3—FREQUENTLY		

1. I feel detached from myself and others.

   1   2   3   4   5   6   7

2. I feel numb inside.

   1   2   3   4   5   6   7

3. I feel shut down.

   1   2   3   4   5   6   7

4. I feel dead inside.

   1   2   3   4   5   6   7

5. I feel a vague inner numbness.

   1   2   3   4   5   6   7

6. I feel out of touch with myself.

   1   2   3   4   5   6   7

7. I feel like there is nothing inside me.

   1   2   3   4   5   6   7

TOTAL _____

Reprinted by permission of the authors: Richard Buggs, Ph.D., Juergen Korbana, Ph.D., Matthew McKay, Ph.D., and Peter D. Rogers, Ph.D.

Research using the Haight Ashbury Mood Scale shows that people reporting higher levels of emptiness tend to have shorter-lived friendships and romantic relationships. For that reason, if you score below 26 on the scale, you should consider trying the following action plans.

Action Plan #1

This is for the partner who scored below 26 on the emptiness questionnaire. If your partner is unwilling to do the exercise, use it as a way to help you draw him or her out in future conversations.

Bear in mind that this can be very tricky territory: people don't like to be pushed beyond where they feel emotionally safe. Try to stay attuned to your partner's reactions, including body language, during your attempts to draw him or her out. Be willing to back off—don't try to be your partner's therapist. Both of you may feel more comfortable doing these exercises with the help of a professional. But if your partner seems curious and interested in trying, use the guidelines below to explore his or her feelings.

Look back at the last three times you experienced empty feelings. Describe to your partner (or on paper) the circumstances that triggered each episode. Talk about how long the feelings lasted and what you did to cope. In as much detail as possible, describe the feelings themselves.

Now collaborate to come up with a name for those feelings—it can be something funny or silly that you both like. Guy came up with the idea of saying "Code Blue" to Danielle. Promise each other that when you notice the feelings, you'll say something or use your signal. This will assure that you can immediately implement action plan #2.

Action Plan #2

It's not important that your partner even buys into the idea of emptiness. This action plan is something you can do together whenever you sense that your partner's behaviors or attitudes are coming out of feelings of emptiness.

Working together, brainstorm a list of ways you could, as partners, strengthen your connection and closeness. Start with anything that seems to have helped in the past, then list as many new ideas as you can think of. Be creative. Don't be afraid to be outrageous.

As you make the list, draw ideas from different categories of experience:

- Things you can do with friends
- Sensual or sexual experiences
- Things that will challenge or excite you
- Activities that will tap into your creativity
- Activities that will deepen your relationship
- Experiences that will give you a feeling of freedom and/or novelty
- Activities that will distract or entertain you

Once you've generated the list, cut it down to the six best items. Note that some ideas may be enhanced or combined, some may be impractical or just not very effective. Eliminate any ideas that, if carried out, would harm someone or get you into serious trouble.

Then commit to using one of the six ideas whenever your partner seems to be struggling with empty feelings.

PART II

◆

The Masking Issues

No one has ever come into my office for couple's therapy and announced that they are afraid of engulfment, abandonment, shame, or emptiness. The presenting issues, or the *masking issues*, as we call them, always have to do with much more practical, everyday matters. "This man is a workaholic." "She's a spendthrift!" "Her need to have a child has hijacked our romantic life." "We never have sex any more." "I can't live another day with his mother!" "She's cheating." "He never talks to me."

In Part I we covered the four fears that are so often at the root of commitment problems. In the next six chapters, we'll present the struggles of six couples who uncovered these fears in the course of their therapy. They didn't necessarily overcome them. What was crucial for them was learning to identify these fears and the ways in which they were sabotaging their relationships.

At the end of each chapter, you'll have the opportunity to do some exercises—either with your partner or alone—that may help you recognize how one or more of these fears have activated the conflicts and disappointments of your own relationships, past and present. The exercises offer strategies for overcoming—or at least coping with—your fears and/or your partner's fears.

The book's last chapter, "Making a Decision: Letting Go Versus Going for It," will help you evaluate whether your relationship, as it functions now, is worth the struggle.

Not all relationships have a long-term future. If they did, humankind would not go through the endlessly colorful, heady, and sometimes humiliating process of trying to find true love. All we can hope for, in the end, is that with each attempt we become a little wiser, making decisions that are more and more likely to lead to what we want.

5

Time

Spending It Together, Spending It Apart

Heather and Tim walked through the door of my consulting room with the shell-shocked, sleep-deprived look one often sees in the faces of first-time parents who are trying to get everything right but fear they're doing everything wrong.

Heather held the baby in a front pack and was carrying a diaper bag big enough to hold all the equipment one would need to climb Mt. Everest. Tim was carrying what looked like either an industrial-strength breast pump or a small bomb. He was also toting his laptop and, with some obvious distress to his masculine pride, Heather's flower-printed shoulder bag.

The couple, both in their mid-thirties, looked much older and more haggard than they should have. Tim needed a shave and looked as if he'd slept in his clothes. Heather was doing her best to cover with the front pack a big wet spot on her blouse. The baby was very beautiful, from what little of her I could see.

I remembered Heather from a group of psychology interns I'd lectured several years back. She'd stood out then for her mental agility, keen perceptions, and the ardor with which she approached her calling. Now she looked like someone who had been undone by life and was barely hanging on.

From the way that she and Tim were avoiding each other's eyes, I gathered that they'd just been fighting. The baby, oblivious to her parents' struggles, was fast asleep and making little sucking noises.

Tim was the one who had called me. A computer animator and general high-tech whiz, he had struck me on the phone as a thoughtful and articulate man who had a good grasp of what was happening to him and Heather, even as parenthood sent them careening into an abyss of conjugal unhappiness.

Time was the issue. Now that they had a baby to take care of in addition to their careers, there just wasn't enough of it to go around. Adding to the normal strains of new parenthood, the baby was colicky, which meant that none of them had had more than two hours of sleep at a stretch since the baby's birth.

Heather, who, like me, is a therapist, knew exactly what was going on with her. She felt overwhelmed, hopeless, and exhausted. She and Tim had enjoyed a warm, loving, and supportive relationship when they set up house together, but all their closeness had gone out the window with the leisure time they used to share. Heather now had frequent fantasies of leaving Tim.

They were both people accustomed to working hard to achieve their goals and seemed utterly bewildered that now—even though they were both working harder than they ever had in their lives—their work ethic and their stubborn determination were suddenly insufficient. Their relationship, their friendship, their plans for a future together were all unraveling before their tired eyes.

My heart went out to them. I wished I could wave a magic wand and grant each of them eight hours of sleep. Lacking a wand to wave, I invited them to come in and sit down.

Heather and Tim's Commitment Dialogue

Dr. McKay: When you called, you talked about being in crisis. I'd like to hear a little bit from each of you about what the crisis is for you right now.

Heather: As you can see, we've got our hands full—literally! We've got this darling little baby. This is something I've wanted for a long time in my life. It's wonderful that we have this child. But I'm just feeling overwhelmed—not only by everything I have to do with the baby. I've also started seeing clients again. And I just don't feel that Tim is there for me, and I really need him now!

Dr. McKay: He's not there for you in what way?

Heather: I need a lot of support right now. I need to feel like Tim is my friend now—that he's going to be there for me. Not only to help with the baby; he does that. But *I* want time with him! I want him to spend time with *me*. I need nurturing, too.

Dr. McKay: What specifically would you like Tim to be doing with you that would nurture you and the relationship?

Heather: I know we have this three-month-old baby, and she doesn't sleep a lot, at least not yet. But we do have help. We do have a really good support network. And I'd like it if we could spend more time together, maybe have a night once a week when we go out. This has been like the death of intimacy in our relationship. I know, okay, I've just had a baby, and I'm a little hormonally overrun right now. But I didn't expect that I was going to lose my companion, my friend. My lover. We don't even talk about anything but diapers and the diaper service and pumping—it's all, *all* about the baby. And I just feel lost in this.

Dr. McKay: Okay—now, Tim. What's your side of the crisis? What's happening for you? Are you concerned about changes that have occurred since the baby arrived?

Tim: Yeah! I feel that there is just zero time for me. Zero time.

Dr. McKay: Zero time for you to do what?

Tim: Just to do my thing—one, to do my work. I'm staying up until all hours trying to get my work done, my normal work. The only time I have alone to even think is when I'm driving into the city. I work like seventy hours a week! It's nuts.

Dr. McKay: So you only have time for work.

Tim: I don't have time for anything that feeds *me*—like these new animations I want to work on. This is a field where you've got to stay on the cutting edge. And then there's the rest of life. I'd love to just be able to read a book once in a while! And that's about as remote a possibility for me now as walking on Mars.

Dr. McKay: So you're concerned that there's no time for you to do creative things, for you to fulfill the work demands that are placed on you or even to just escape into a good novel.

Tim: I am so sleep deprived now that if I just sit down with a book, I read about two sentences and I'm asleep. That's on a good night.

Dr. McKay: So the two of you really have very different needs right now. Heather, you are hoping to hold on to a feeling of closeness with Tim, and you feel it slipping away, particularly since the baby arrived. There just doesn't seem to be any time set aside for the two of you to find that spark together. And, Tim, on your end, there's a feeling you've sort of lost yourself here—the time you need to work, to think, to create, to just rest and read. That's all disappeared. And what I want to look at right now is how that affects you emotionally. Heather, when you start feeling this kind of yearning to have a nourishing relationship with Tim, something that feels close and loving, and it just doesn't happen—what's the feeling that comes up?

Heather: I feel really sad! Actually I've been feeling really, really depressed lately. It's almost feeling out of control.

Dr. McKay: Is there any other feeling that comes up besides sadness?

Heather: I don't know. The sadness has been pretty overwhelming.

Dr. McKay: But when you feel like you can't reach Tim, when he's withdrawn into the computer or a book or some other private space and you can't reach him, what's the feeling that comes up? There's sadness. Is there anything else?

Heather: Kind of panic.

Dr. McKay: Panic.

Heather: Yeah, it's fear.

Dr. McKay: What scares you when you see Tim just kind of going through the motions, taking care of things you need him to do and then as quickly as he can, shifting into these private activities?

Heather: I don't want to lose him! It just feels like he's going to leave. I keep thinking that's what he's thinking about. Even when we're together, I just see this look in his eyes. I keep thinking he's thinking about leaving.

Dr. McKay: It's a very scary thought—particularly when you have a three-month-old baby. And maybe not being married makes it even scarier.

Heather: I think that's true.

Dr. McKay: Tim, Heather is scared that you might leave. And I guess I'm wondering about this struggle you have to find more time for yourself. When you can't get enough of that time alone, time to think, time to read, time to work on computer animations, what do you feel then?

Tim: This is something I think I've been struggling with just about as long as I can remember. I've just always been fighting against other people sucking my time. Needing me to do things for them. Needing to take care of things for them. It was like that even when I was a kid. I'm the oldest of five kids, and my parents just always looked to me as the one who'd take care of the little ones, see that things were going along, being there when they got home from school. And I never had enough time! I have never had enough time.

Dr. McKay: So what's happening in your family right now is just a continuation of a long, long pattern of struggling to have enough time and space for yourself.

Tim: It is! I mean, that's what I thought I was getting away from when I got to grow up and move out. I thought I was getting away from all that. And here I am, right back in it again. Actually, I just can't believe it. And, really, it doesn't have anything to do with

Heather. It's not personal. This just wasn't part of my plan. But, Heather and I were together, and she got pregnant. It was a surprise to both of us. I wanted to support her in this, be there for her. But I don't really think I thought it through, about what it would really mean. I just feel like this has thrown me straight back into the worst aspects of my own childhood.

Dr. McKay: So here you feel like you're taking care of your siblings again, and your life gets lost somehow.

Tim: Yeah! And now Heather wants me to take care of her, too! I just feel like there's nothing left for me.

Dr. McKay: And when you have that feeling that there's nothing left for you, there's no room for Tim here, what's the emotion that goes with that?

Tim: I just feel that I need to protect myself. I feel like I need to withdraw to a place where I can remember who I am. Because if I don't, I am just going to lose who I am.

Dr. McKay: And if you don't withdraw to that place, where you know who you are, what do you feel like?

Tim: I feel like I'm being colonized, like I'm being taken over. Like there is going to be nothing left of me. It's scary.

Dr. McKay: So both of you are scared. But you're scared about different things. Heather, you're scared that this relationship that's so important to you is somehow in danger, and you may end up alone. You have a panicky feeling about that. And, Tim, you're afraid that you're being colonized, taken over, losing yourself. These are both very terrifying inner experiences. Let me ask you something, Heather. Is this loss of someone important and significant to you something that you've gone through before in your life? Has that been part of your history?

Heather: Yes.

Dr. McKay: How so?

Heather: It's kind of the classic setup. My mom was a very emotionally shut down person. I was very close to my dad. He was the parent I really identified with, or wanted to identify with. And then he left. He left when I was five. He got married again, and he started a new family. And their firstborn was this beautiful golden girl who was smart and pretty and lively and fun, and he just adored her. And I just always felt that somehow I never measured up.

Dr. McKay: What happened to your relationship to your father, after he started his new family?

Heather: Well, you know, I got the crumbs, the crusts from him. He'd blow into town once in a while and take me out for a movie and dinner and ice cream, and maybe he'd buy me a new dress or new shoes. He'd kind of spoil me a little, and I'd remember all those wonderful feelings about being his girl. I'd feel so proud.

Dr. McKay: And then he'd be gone.

Heather: And then he'd be gone. And I knew, those other kids, they had him all the time. He had pictures of them in his wallet, and he'd always say, "Look at your brothers and sister." But he never took me to see them. And I didn't really want to have anything to do with them anyway. I just wanted him back. And that was never going to happen. He was never going to come back. It left a hole in my heart.

Dr. McKay: So you have a very real fear that comes from very real experiences—losing this parent who was so important to you and ending up having to live with a detached, disconnected, unavailable mother. And this charming, interesting, fun father going away and only occasionally seeing you, only occasionally bringing you some sunshine.

Heather: My biggest fear was that somehow, because I was left behind with my mother, I was like her or destined to become like her—the dull one, the one who was going to be abandoned, the one who couldn't hold the interest of another person.

Dr. McKay: And you're afraid that's happening now with Tim.

Heather: Well, look at it! Look at what's happening.

Heather and Tim have gotten down to their core issues very quickly. Their pain is right on the surface; the fear is easily identified. Heather is scared that she's going to repeat her childhood, lose the man she cares about. She fears that she has become boring and uninteresting like her mother and will soon be abandoned. Tim is scared that he's going to repeat his childhood—taking care of children, losing himself, suffering real engulfment as he struggles to balance the needs of a family with the extraordinary time commitments of his job and need to take care of his own creativity and interests.

They're both in a real bind, because, in truth, at this point in their lives, there isn't enough time for everything. There is not enough time for Tim to fully take care of his need for an independent self. And there's not enough time for the kind of intimacy and interpersonal nourishment that Heather is hoping to reestablish in their relationship. So we're going to have to do the best we can with limited time and limited energy and two people who are terribly afraid that they're about to descend into the nightmares of their respective childhoods.

Dr. McKay: I want to ask you both a difficult question, and I'd like to hear each of you answer it. I know you're feeling scared in this relationship. But I also want to be clear: Are you here today because you really want to change and make the relationship better? Do you want to commit to the work you'll need to do to get the relationship back on track?

Heather: Those are hard questions to answer. I guess I have to admit that lately—I don't know whether it's hormones or what—sometimes, I just can't stand it. It's like waiting for the gun to fire. I keep thinking that he's going to leave anyway, and I just want to get it over with. I just want to be by myself with the baby, if that's how it's going to be. If I'm going to end up being a single mom, then I'd rather just get on with it.

Dr. McKay: So a part of you is really scared that it's falling apart and might even prefer to just reach a point where you can be on your own and not have to go through the process of feeling everything disintegrate?

Heather: That's the feeling I get when I get that sense of panic. I swear, lately I've been feeling like one of my own most helpless patients—someone who has some intractable relationship problem that they just can't work through. There doesn't seem to be a happy ending or a resolution, and I don't know how to help them. And that's kind of how I'm feeling now. I don't know; I can't see the way out sometimes.

Dr. McKay: So you're feeling a lot of discouragement. I want to get back to those questions. In spite of the discouragement and the thoughts that maybe you'd just be better off getting it over with and being alone, are you ready to do some work and put in some effort to really get the relationship back on track?

Heather: I am—of course I am. I'm desperate for it!

Dr. McKay: Tim, I want to ask you the same question. I know you're scared and feeling like you're going to lose yourself, and you need time alone and you don't have enough of it, and you're feeling very pressured by the demands of a new baby and also Heather's need for closeness. But I want to ask you, are you ready to work together— to really roll up your sleeves and make changes to improve the relationship? Are you willing to commit to that?

Tim: I would if I could see light at the end of the tunnel, if I could think of this as an intense job but one that's finite. I need to feel like I'll eventually get to the end of it and then I'll have some time. But if it seems like something that's just going to go on and on and on forever . . .

Dr. McKay: It's scary to think that it might be interminable. And in reality, just to respond to that fear head-on, this first year especially is going to be tough. Maybe even these first couple of years. But then things will get easier. They do get easier after a while. This is a highly intense time, and it demands a tremendous amount of energy and dedication from both of you. But things eventually do get a little easier, and more time opens up later on. So we need to focus on strategies for getting through a couple of very challenging years and, more immediately, getting through the next couple of months, and doing so in a way that addresses both of your needs.

Tim: I'm used to that kind of thing. I'm used to crazy, impossible deadlines and having to work around the clock trying to meet them. I can do it. I can put in a big effort. I can work hard—I know that.

Dr. McKay: So going back to that question about you and Heather. You know about how to push yourself to meet a deadline and how to really try to make something happen. Is that something you're willing to do now, with her? Are you willing to use our therapy time to make the changes necessary for the relationship to work?

Tim: Sometimes when I'm feeling so completely overwhelmed, I might answer no to that question. But I look down at this beautiful baby and I think, "How can I say anything but yes?" Yes!

Dr. McKay: So the commitment is to the baby. But I also want to know about your commitment to Heather.

Tim: It's to Heather! It's absolutely to Heather.

Dr. McKay: And why is that? Why do you have a commitment to Heather?

Tim: Because Heather's my partner. We share something very important. I feel like nobody in the world understands me as well as she does. And probably nobody else in the world would put up with me, except her.

Dr. McKay: So in spite of this very difficult time, a time when you feel this looming sense of losing yourself, of not having any time to take care of yourself, you have a commitment to Heather and you want to make this relationship work.

Tim: That's why I called you.

Dr. McKay: Heather, what happens for you when you hear Tim say that he has a commitment to this relationship, that he wants to make it work?

Heather: I want to believe him! I have to admit I feel a little surprised to hear Tim say that right now, just because of the vibe I've been getting from him—that look I see in his eyes when we're together, that he would just rather be by himself, doing his own stuff; that he doesn't want to be with me. I'm glad to hear him say it; I'm not sure I totally believe it. I believe that he thinks he believes it. But I'm not sure that's coming from deep inside him.

Dr. McKay: So you have a little cautious hope, but you'll need to see how this unfolds.

Heather: Well, the proof's in the pudding, isn't it?

Once we have a commitment to work on the critical problems facing this couple, we need to continue to frame the initial challenge as getting through several difficult months. We're going to focus on what is necessary to get through the next few months—because if we look at eighteen years of raising a child, Tim is going to be overwhelmed. So we're going to reduce the challenge to the few months lying ahead, and we're going to develop a set of specific agreements to help both Tim and Heather navigate this difficult time.

Dr. McKay: I want to talk to you about something that is tremendously important and creates a foundation for couples that succeed. And it's the idea of what I call equally valid needs—that each person in the partnership has very critically important needs. And no solution to a relationship problem will work that doesn't in some way address and incorporate at least some of each person's needs. Tim, you need time for yourself, time to breathe, time to create, time to read, time to think. Heather, you need to feel a strengthened bond with Tim. You need to feel closeness, a sense of the integrity of your relationship, that it really is something that's nurturing you and your family. These are really important needs, and they tend to draw you in different directions. You need time together, Heather, and Tim is desperate for a little time alone—and it's very hard. But these are both valid needs.

Heather: That really makes a lot of sense. But in our situation, our equally valid needs are diametrically opposed. How in the world can we find reconciliation between two such different things, these opposites, where he needs time alone and I need time together? I just don't see a meeting place.

Dr. McKay: I hear you loud and clear. And it's true—there's not enough time for each of you to have all of what you need. There's not enough time right now for a vibrant, intense, highly intimate relationship. And there isn't enough time for Tim to develop all of the computer animation projects he would like to be working on and read and think and have time for himself. But our work is to find time that will allow each of you to get some of what you need while at the same time keeping this family going, taking care of your baby, and nurturing this relationship.

Heather: That sounds fair enough.

Dr. McKay: What about you, Tim? Does this idea make sense to you?

Tim: Yeah, it does make sense to me. It makes a lot of sense. It sounds like a project with a deadline, where we're really pushing to get the work done and all the energy for the moment has to go into that project, and you put some of your other needs on hold.

Dr. McKay: So we're going to try to figure out how to create structures in your relationship that will allow each of you to get some of what you hunger for. Over the next couple of months we will need to really look at the time that each of you has, and how we can restructure that time so that at least some of these very important needs are better met. And any solution we decide on has to be a solution that the two of you arrive at together. It has to be the couple's solution. And any compromise we create has to be something you develop together. There can't be winners and losers in this. There can't be someone getting their needs met and somebody still hungry, someone feeling like their needs are being ignored. That'll never work. So we're going to have to work together. The two of you will be the primary architects of the plan we'll create to get through these next few months.

So I'd like to hear from each of you. What changes could be made to the way time functions in your relationship so that some of the needs each of you described could be better taken care of?

Tim: Well, one thing that I can think of right away is I think we could change the way we think about child care. We're paying for twenty hours a week. And we've used that time mostly so Heather can see clients or run errands, or so she can go out and have some time by herself or do something fun. But if we could think of that child care in a different way, maybe as a way to also address some of these needs that each of us has, maybe it could buy some alone time for me, and maybe it could buy some "together" time for Heather and me. And maybe we need to add five hours a week.

Dr. McKay: So your suggestion would be to maybe use a few hours a week of the child care for taking care of your needs—more alone time for you and some more together time for Heather. What do you think, Heather? Do you have any ideas?

Heather: I think if I had a sense that we could reserve one evening a week for us together, for intimate time—maybe going out to dinner together, maybe going out to a concert or to see a movie or a play . . . just something that would be really time for us together. Or even just an evening alone together in bed, knowing that we won't be disturbed.

Dr. McKay: So you're kind of piggybacking on Tim's child care idea, of using some child care to have a night out and do things together and reconnect emotionally and romantically?

Heather: It would be really nice. But I guess when we have tried to do that stuff, I just have this nagging feeling. I see this look in Tim's eyes, like he really would rather be by himself. And it just kind of kills it for me. You know, it's almost like I can't be there enjoying the time, because I keep thinking that he doesn't want to be there. And I think it makes me kind of withdraw, and then I become that boring person I'm afraid he's going to reject.

Dr. McKay: Tim, do you have any thoughts about that?

Tim: Well, there's a certain amount of truth to it, because I'm not getting the time I need. But if I were getting that time—if I could look forward to a block of four hours or even two hours that I could have to myself, without feeling guilty about it . . . And if I know that Heather is getting her needs met at some other time . . . or maybe even with other people! Well, I guess that wouldn't do it. But if I didn't have to feel guilty about my time, I could enjoy it more thoroughly and get more nourishment from it, too.

Dr. McKay: So you feel like you could really be there and really be fully present and fully participating in that moment with Heather if you had a little bit of time with yourself.

Tim: Yeah, because right now there's this finite quantity of time, and we're both just grabbing at it.

Dr. McKay: You're scraping to try and get little bits and pieces for yourself. Heather, what happens for you when you hear Tim say that he feels like he could really be present and really enjoy the time together if he had a little bit of alone time to give him that sense of personal space that he needs?

Heather: I want to believe him. I think I've just got so much baggage with this issue that it would probably help me to be hit over the head with this a little bit while he's with me. Maybe he could just tell me, I'm glad to be with you right now. I think I need that reassurance.

Dr. McKay: So is that something that feels possible—to give Heather a little reassurance?

Tim: Yeah—why not? I'll be as explicit as she needs me to be. Heather knows I'm no good at lying. So if I say something like that to her, she knows it's the truth.

Dr. McKay: Okay, let's roll up our sleeves right now and get down to the specifics of what we're going to do, how much time you're going to have for each other romantically in a week, how much time Tim is going to get, how you're going to use the child care to set that up. We're going to get down to the nuts and bolts of this and set up an experiment and see over the next few weeks how that works.

Later we'll have to evaluate how it's going and make any necessary changes and adjustments as we go along.

Therapist's Overview

Conflicts over time and attention can become intensely polarized for many couples. Repeated often enough, the issue becomes very painful—a familiar path full of sharp rocks and broken glass.

Time is a charged issue for one reason—it taps into core needs. The hunger for connection and human nourishment; the need to be seen and known. But also the need for autonomy, for a private self that seeks experiences outside the relationship.

There are corresponding fears that also have a great influence on a couple's relationship to time they spend together and apart. The fear of loss and abandonment can surface when you get less time than you need with a partner. Time is like oxygen for a relationship. When there's too little of it, the relationship starts to suffocate; a partner can become desperate for attention and intimacy. The fear of abandonment can escalate as the hunger for closeness intensifies.

A second fear associated with conflicts over time is engulfment. Partners struggling with engulfment experience time devoted to the relationship as a lost opportunity to take care of themselves. Needs for friendship and camaraderie, for time alone to create or think or decompress, for favorite sports and recreations, for a moment free of demands and expectations can easily be swept aside by a close relationship. It can seem that there's no room for an independent self that seeks nourishment outside the world created by the couple.

Heather and Tim's battle over time is fueled by these classic fears of loss and engulfment. Their struggle has started to harden into what family therapists call a *pursuer-distancer system*. As one partner demands more time and attention, the other tends to withdraw. The pursuer-distancer system is both painful and predictive of future breakup. John Gottman, the foremost researcher in marriage longevity, has found that frequent demand-withdrawal interactions not only strain relationships but also greatly increase the chances that partners will eventually give up.

Conflicts over time can feel like they have very high stakes when one or both partners have committed to a major life challenge. Heather and Tim's baby is one example. But there are many others. Going back to school, taking on new job responsibilities, or starting a major creative project are all likely to raise issues about time.

Two other fears we've explored in this book, the fear of emptiness and the fear of shame, may also show up in struggles over time and attention. But they do so less often. People who fear shame will sometimes restrict the time given to a relationship, because they fear being truly known. Intimate moments are scary because a partner might come to recognize one's hidden flaws or see the shameful damage from a childhood laced with rejection and abuse.

The fear of emptiness may sometimes lurk behind a conflict over time. When a partner doesn't feel seen and intimately connected, the hunger for closeness may become an ache. And that ache may be experienced as a lonely or empty feeling. For some people, this emptiness is terrifying. It sends them back to the dark, helpless days of childhood when no one saw their pain, when no one came when they called.

If you and your partner keep getting stuck over issues of time, one of the key fears we've just discussed—fear of abandonment, engulfment, emptiness, or shame—may be a contributing factor. You and your partner need to stop arguing about time and look at the underlying issues fueling the conflict. We suggest using the Couples Research Form that follows to explore the critical fears each of you may be bringing to the issue of time.

Couples Research Form

Issue/Conflict: _____

Fears: *What does my partner fear might happen?* _____
_____

Other feelings my partner has about this issue: _____

_____

History: *What are my partner's experiences from the past (this or other relationships, or childhood experiences) that relate to this issue?* _____

_____

Assumptions: *What are my partner's beliefs about this issue — about what will happen in the future; about my motives, feelings, and intentions?* _____

_____

Perceived choices: *What options does my partner believe he or she has regarding this issue?* _____

_____

Needs: *What does my partner want and need?* _____

_____

Adapted from *When Anger Hurts Your Relationship* by Kim Paleg, Ph.D., and Matthew McKay, Ph.D. Used by permission.

You can do this exercise with your partner if your partner is willing to participate. The exercise will still be useful if you do it alone. In that case, fill out the form twice, once as it applies to yourself and once as you feel your partner would respond.

Start by each writing a one- or two-sentence description of the problem on a separate piece of paper. "Our disagreements about how much time to spend together and apart" is an example of a description that's simple and neutral. It is important to use nonblaming language.

Let your partner read and rewrite your description, if necessary, to make it more accurately incorporate both of your points of view. (Obviously, this won't be necessary if you're doing the exercise by yourself.) The goal is to craft a short, simple statement that's neutral and accurate. Continue this process, passing your draft back and forth until you achieve a statement of the conflict that's acceptable to both of you.

At this point, go ahead and begin the actual interview exercise. It doesn't matter which of you goes first; you'll each get a turn at interviewing and being interviewed.

Starting with *fears*, ask your partner:

- What are you afraid might happen if our time was spent more in the way I want us to spend it?
- Do you have any worries about what might happen if I got my way on this issue?
- Do you have any fears about what might happen if we can't eventually agree on this issue?

Moving to the *other feelings* section, ask your partner some or all of the following:

- Do you have other feelings that are triggered by how we spend our time?
- What feelings would you have if things stayed as they are now, in terms of time spent together and apart?
- What's the most difficult feeling that comes up for you around this issue?

In terms of *history*, ask your partner one or more of these questions:

- What experiences have you had in past relationships that affect your feelings about how we spend time in ours?
- Is there anything that's happened between us that strongly influences how you feel about this issue?

- Were there periods in the past during which you felt suffocated because a relationship took time that you needed for your own life?
- Have you had experiences in which you couldn't get enough attention from your partner and/or time together in a relationship?

Under *assumptions*, ask the following:

- How do you see our conflicts about time? What's the part of your point of view that didn't get included in our neutral description?
- What's your sense of what makes me feel the way I do about this issue?

Regarding *perceived choices*, try some of these questions:

- What choices do we have with this issue?
- Are there any options open to us that might help us resolve this conflict?
- Is any compromise available to us in terms of things we do together versus our individual needs?

Under *needs*, ask your partner:

- What are your needs in this issue?
- What's the most important thing you need in terms of time together or apart?
- If things were exactly the way you want them, what would that look like?

Make sure, while doing the interview, to write down the main responses your partner gave to every question. Stay away from correcting, refuting, judging, or commenting on what your partner says. Just pretend you're a journalist trying to get the facts. You may not agree with everything your partner says, but it is important that you try to understand it. If you're working by yourself, try to be as honest and as unbiased as you can, summoning as much empathy as you can for your partner's point of view.

As soon as the interview is complete, reverse the process. The interviewer becomes the interviewee and answers all the questions he or she just asked. (Or, if you're working alone, fill out the form as close as you can to how you think your partner would answer the questions.)

When you've completed the exercise with the Couples Research Form, whether working with your partner or alone, you'll have a lot of new information and perhaps some new insights about your partner's feelings and needs. Knowledge builds respect. The more you learn about each other's desires and emotional needs, the better equipped you'll be to face conflicts with empathy rather than blame.

Principle of Equally Valid Needs

It's very important to note here that the needs that each of you has identified and expressed, though very different, are absolutely legitimate, valid, and reasonable. Trying to minimize or negate your partner's needs, shame or blame them, or in any way talk them out of what they want is a losing strategy. Over the long term, this behavior will lead to resentment and stalemate. It is much more effective to use what you know about each other's needs to develop a new collaborative solution to your problem.

Mapping the Week

When you each have an hour to spare, sit down separately to schedule what you consider to be an ideal week—what you'd like to do with your nonwork time.

Divide a piece of paper into seven vertical columns, each for a day of the week. In the left margin, write the waking hours of the day—maybe 7:00 A.M. at the top going down to 11:00 P.M. or midnight at the bottom. Now, for each hour that you're not working or doing chores, pencil in how you'd like to spend that time. Some entries will consist of only a word or two—gardening, tennis, watching TV, reading, yoga. Others will need more description—walking the dog, tinkering with my motorcycle, movie and dinner with [insert your partner's name], or bicycle ride with [insert your partner's name].

Notice the ratio of time spent with your partner versus activities you do alone or with others. Does this feel about right? Would you like to adjust it? If you want to make any changes, just erase an entry and fill in something else. Have you reserved enough time for activities (hobbies, sports, recreation, creative or cultural experiences) that are important to you? Does your week feel balanced? Keep making adjustments as necessary.

Now comes an important moment. Share your map of the week with each other. Ask questions. Talk about some of your concerns and priorities about time. Discuss your sense of the ideal balance between time spent together and time spent apart. Try not to get angry or withdraw if you feel hurt or disappointed by how your partner has arranged his or her week. Instead, just keep asking questions, trying to learn all you can about what your partner needs and values.

Now there's one more thing to do. Make a new seven-column map of the week. This time, work together to create a schedule that the two of you agree on. Start with time you want to share, such as cooking and eating dinner, cuddle time in front of the TV, attending sports or cultural activities, and recreation you want to do together. Then fill in your independent activities. Discuss your reactions to the exercise. Does the week feel balanced? Is there enough time together? Apart? Explore possible compromises. Then erase and make changes in the schedule to reflect your new ideas.

This exercise will help you explore some of the differences in how you and your partner approach time, opening the door to creating a healthy and mutually satisfying balance between the time you spend together and the time you spend apart.

6

Money

Yours, Mine, and Ours

Iris spoke volumes in the first sentences she uttered after introducing herself on the telephone. "My father's a florist." I recognized the name of the flower shop—there are several billboards advertising it around town. "He named all of us—all five of his daughters—for flowers. But it didn't help him much, because I was the only one that stayed on in the shop—the only one too dumb to go on to something else, I guess."

Iris got pregnant, she told me, in her junior year of high school. It was a crisis for everyone involved. But Iris's parents rose to the occasion, offering to support Iris and help her raise the baby while she finished high school and earned a degree at the local junior college.

Continuing to live in her childhood room (the baby inherited one of her sister's bedrooms), Iris dutifully studied for a certificate in accounting while working part-time for no pay in her father's flower shop. She had a flair for making bouquets, and she was good with the customers.

Her most devoted customer was a young real estate agent named Gregory, who had taken to filling whatever house he was showing with beautiful arrangements of cut flowers from the shop. He always praised Iris extravagantly for her work, and tipped her, too. Soon she was spending her Thursday and Sunday mornings helping Gregory place her flower arrangements in homes scheduled for open houses. He told her she was his good luck charm—whatever house she walked into, he sold for more than the asking price.

At first Iris's father was resistant to the idea of Gregory's courtship. He said there was something he didn't like about Gregory's open-handed style. "He's too wild in the way he spends money," Iris's father told her. "Like a gambler. You want someone solid, honey. Someone who's going to know how to take care of a wife and a family."

But Gregory's kindness to Iris's child—now a first-grader—won everyone over. He always brought gifts for her if he came to eat dinner with the family. He joked with Iris's married sisters and made Iris's mother promise to teach Iris how to cook everything he ate at her table. A couple of times, he invited the entire extended family out for dinner on his tab. "It's my turn," he told Iris's dad, who refrained from commenting on Gregory's choice of pricey restaurants until his future son-in-law was safely out of earshot. "What is he, a drug dealer or something, to have that kind of money?" he said in the kitchen later to Iris and her mom.

"He just sold a house!" Iris told him.

"Well, he should put some of that money away instead of spending it all the minute he gets it."

Even though she didn't dare say anything about it to her father, Iris was quite taken by Gregory's extravagant generosity. It was so different from her mother and father's cautious, tightfisted approach to life. It made her feel special, she said—like maybe she wasn't such a hopeless screwup after all.

As so often happens, the very qualities Iris found so charming in Gregory at the start of their relationship turned out to be the same characteristics that caused her anguish later on. She and Gregory got married and had two children in quick succession, a boy and a girl. Iris, out of a sense of filial duty, continued to work in her father's shop, although now he paid her minimum wage, the same wage he paid his other florists. "It's only fair," he told Iris.

But the housing market slumped and all of a sudden Gregory wasn't bringing home the bacon anymore. Instead of tightening their belts, as Iris's upbringing and professional training urged her to do, Gregory insisted that they continue to live just the same as before. "If you look like you're hurting, pretty soon everyone thinks you're a loser," he told Iris. "We owe it to ourselves, and we owe it to the kids, to keep up appearances, even if we have to live on credit for a little while, until the market picks up again."

Iris's first daughter went to the same Catholic school Iris and her sisters had attended. Even after Iris and her child moved out of her parents' house, Iris's father continued to quietly foot the bill. But Gregory, who wasn't Catholic, had insisted on sending their two kids, a girl and a boy, to the local public school. Iris felt like she was failing her children and failing her parents because her second and third child were being left out of this family tradition. But she also knew that she and Gregory simply didn't earn enough money to send all three of their kids to private school.

All hell broke loose when Iris's father, discreetly enough, offered to pay. "What does he think?" Gregory fumed at Iris, "That I'm some sort of bum who can't take care of his own family? Maybe if he paid you more than minimum wage we'd have a little more wiggle room in our budget here."

The sad truth, Iris knew, was that they didn't have a budget. Every time she proposed one to Gregory, he'd blow up at her. "You know what the trouble is with you, Iris?" he'd yell. "You think too small. You gotta think big if you're gonna make it."

Gregory left it to Iris every month to pay the bills. She made whatever economies she could without inviting Gregory's criticism, but there was more than one occasion when she went to her father for help. She made her father swear that he would never say anything to her husband.

By the time Iris and Gregory came to see me, both their financial and their marital situation had spun completely out of control.

Iris and Gregory's Commitment Dialogue

Dr. McKay: Iris, I know that you and Gregory have been struggling with money issues, and I'd like to understand a little better how that plays out between you. How are you conflicted about money?

Iris: We just seem to look at it in very different ways. I thought, when we got married, that we had the same values and goals, but the longer we're together the more I realize that we just don't see eye to eye.

Dr. McKay: How does Gregory want to use money that's different from you?

Iris: I just feel like he's not realistic about it. The way he spends it doesn't seem to be relative to what we have.

Dr. McKay: Let's not look at it in terms of whether it's realistic or not, or right or wrong. What are you observing? What's happening with money that concerns you?

Iris: I'm the one who pays the bills every month, and it's a juggling act every month. At this point, even though we have two incomes, we don't have enough to meet our expenses every month. One of our kids is entering first grade, the other is entering kindergarten. The local school where we live isn't any good—it's a rotten school. I want to send my kids to Catholic school. That's how I was raised, in a Catholic school. But we don't have the money to pay the tuition. And it makes me feel like a bad mother! I always assumed my kids would go to Catholic school, just like I went to Catholic school. All my sisters went to Catholic school. But we don't have the money. And yet, at the same time—this month—Gregory came home with this big grin on his face and these huge boxes in the back of his car, and said, "Hey, look! We got this new home entertainment system—this home theater!" I mean, it's this huge thing—and we can't afford that! How can we afford that if we can't afford our kids' tuition?

Dr. McKay: Iris, what does it mean to you if you can't have your kids in a school you think they should be in?

Iris: I feel humiliated! I feel like there's something wrong with me, like I don't deserve to have kids.

Dr. McKay: You feel humiliated. And it feels like you're failing as a parent?

Iris: Yeah.

Dr. McKay: Are other money-related things going on that make you feel like there's something wrong with you?

Iris: Well, you know I work in my dad's shop, and we talk every day. My dad's a successful businessman. He's got a chain of flower shops. And it's great working together—I love my dad. But, of course, he asks me about stuff. "How are things going? How many houses has Gregory sold?" And it makes me feel like we're not measuring up. I feel really embarrassed about the fact that we're having money problems. And there have been a few times when I've asked my dad for an advance on my pay. I've asked for a loan!

Dr. McKay: So what does it mean to you when you have to turn to your dad for help, when you and Gregory don't have enough on your own?

Iris: It's like I'm a kid again, like I never grew up. It makes me feel really horrible.

Dr. McKay: So, again, that embarrassment—that shamed feeling.

Iris: Yeah, I feel really embarrassed.

Dr. McKay: Let me turn to you for a minute, Gregory. How do you see the money issues playing out between you and Iris? What's your perspective on this?

Gregory: I feel like—you know, I can't win! I see myself as a good provider. I want the best for my kids and my wife. I get them nice presents sometimes. I mean, that's what a man does for his family, right?

Dr. McKay: Oftentimes that's exactly right. But I wonder how it is that you spend money that's different from how Iris would prefer.

Gregory: You know, she's kind of a timid person. I think she's still under her father's thumb. She's still worried about what he's going to say all the time.

Iris: Yeah! I'm worried because I have to face the man every day, knowing that I borrowed money from him because we couldn't get by one month. And then we go out to dinner with Mom and Dad, and *you* pick up the tab—like you're Mr. Big Shot. I mean, think how embarrassing that is!

Gregory: What kind of a man is it that can't pick up the tab when he goes out to dinner with his wife and his kids and his in-laws? Iris, think about it! This is important to me.

Dr. McKay: So, Gregory, it's important to you to show your family—including your father-in-law—that you take care of things. You can take care of them. You can be generous. You're a man who's doing okay in the world. Is that right?

Gregory: Yeah, that's right!

Dr. McKay: Let me go back for a minute, Gregory, to that question I asked. How do you want to spend money differently than Iris? You seem to have a slightly different agenda, in terms of what money should do or can do, than Iris does.

Gregory: Well, I think money is for making people happy. I like to buy things to make people happy. I like to do things to make people feel happy. I mean, I bought Iris diamond earrings for her birthday. And she wants me to take them back to the store. She says they're too much. I said, "These are beautiful! These are going to look beautiful on you." And she says, "No, take them back!" Our whole lives are like that. I bought this really nice piano for our daughter, because she's starting to get interested in music. And Iris says, "Take that back! Let's get one of those electric keyboards instead." It's unbelievable to me that she doesn't want us to get a piano for our daughter!

Iris: But, Gregory—let's be real. It's not just the idea of the diamond earrings. It's not just the idea of the piano. Yeah, it would be great to have these things, if we could afford them! But we can't, honey. We can't! If we don't have the money for our basic expenses, then we definitely don't have the money for diamond earrings and a piano. I feel like, with you, all these things say something about *you* to the world. That's what they seem to be about.

Dr. McKay: So, Iris, I understand what you're saying. The feeling you have is that money should be carefully spent and it should be spent on things like the children's education and balancing the budget. And you're very uncomfortable with spending money on very lovely and beautiful gifts.

Iris: I'm totally uncomfortable with spending money we don't have. I'm totally uncomfortable with the idea of getting deeper and deeper into debt!

Gregory: Iris, what you don't understand is that people waste a lot of money buying crap that breaks, that falls apart. I believe, and my father always used to tell me, that you have to buy something that's really well made, that's really excellent. There's no point in buying anything if you can't buy the best, because it'll last you a long time. I wanted to buy our daughter a piano that was really well made, that was really going to last her—that she will still be playing in twenty years.

Iris: That's great. But how are we going to pay for it? If you only want to buy the best, that's fine. But wait until you actually have money for it.

Dr. McKay: Okay, let me just break in and stop you both for a minute. I'm hearing you operating from very, very different values when it comes to the issue of money. Gregory, it's important to you to buy the best. It's important to you to be generous to your wife, to your kids. It's important to be generous to your extended family, especially your father-in-law, to be able to show your appreciation and gratitude by really doing something nice for them, like taking them out for dinner. And so you're spending money to give people things. And you're confused, because Iris is saying she doesn't want to do that. She doesn't want those kinds of gifts, and, really, what she wants is a life where you very carefully husband your resources and spend them on the things she thinks are most important—

Iris: May I break in for a minute here? This is just an example, and it's a really telling example. When Gregory sells a house, he gets a good commission for it. But he turns around and buys an inappropriately expensive present for the people who bought the house. I mean, it's crazy, the presents he gets for these people. He says he wants to make them happy. But it's like he wants to look like a big shot who has a lot of money to throw around. What he makes on those commissions is the main part of what we're living on. It's not tied to reality. It's like some image he has in his mind of who he is, but he's really not!

Gregory: I'm sorry, Iris! You just don't even understand how money supports not just lifestyle but a whole way of being in the world. It's important to be giving.

Iris: You can do that without spending money. You can be generous, you can give of yourself, you can give up your time. But buying expensive gifts for people—it's just irresponsible right now. Do that later! Do that when your career is at some different stage, when you're a broker, when you've got agents working for you.

Dr. McKay: Okay, once again, Iris and Gregory. It's clear that you have very different value systems about money. But I'd like to get a little deeper than that. Iris, when Gregory spends money in ways that feel to him generous but create difficulties for you, how do you feel then? What does it feel like to be in that position?

Iris: It's a horrible feeling. I feel totally embarrassed. I feel like I can't even show my face.

Dr. McKay: Yeah, you said that word before. You feel embarrassed like there's something wrong, something wrong with you.

Iris: I just want to hide.

Dr. McKay: So your core experience when you have to go to your dad for money, when he questions you about how you're using your resources, when you find there's not enough money in the bank to send your kids to school, your feeling is to be ashamed. You feel like you're not doing right, you're not living right.

Iris: I think this is normal. It's normal to feel ashamed when you're not making it work. You're out there, supposedly living as an adult, and you're not making it work.

Now we're starting to learn about Iris's core emotional experience. She's deeply embarrassed, even ashamed, when she has to turn to her father for money, when she has to respond to his questions about what's happening to their family's resources. The shame gets particularly deep when she worries that she won't have the money to send her children to the Catholic school that is part of her heritage. She feels like she's letting them down. She's failing as a parent.

Dr. McKay: Gregory, let me ask you a question. If you couldn't take your father-in-law out to dinner, if you couldn't buy your daughter that really lovely piano you got her, if you couldn't be generous, how would that make you feel?

Gregory: I don't know. I don't know what I'd feel.

Dr. McKay: Let's think about it a little bit more, Gregory. Imagine a life where those gestures are impossible. Where you are no longer able to give to people, to show them your appreciation, to show them how much you value them. Imagine a world where you have to live counting your pennies and being very careful. What happens inside you when you imagine that? What's the feeling then?

Gregory: I feel stupid. I feel like I'm not living right. I know how to live! I know what the point of living is—it's to be generous. It's to take care of people. It's to take care of your family. It's to buy things that you know will last. The point is to care about value. That's what I think about it.

Dr. McKay: Okay, Gregory. You care about value. You care about making sure that your children, your wife, the people in your life experience your generosity.

Gregory: It's not that! It's not that they experience my generosity. It's that they feel good. That's what I care about.

Dr. McKay: Okay, it's that they feel good. And what would happen if you couldn't be that person? What would it feel like if you couldn't be the person who is generous in that way—who helps people feel good? The person who gives them things that will last, that they can really value?

Gregory: I don't know. I guess I'd just feel like I'm letting people down.

Dr. McKay: And if you felt yourself letting people down in that way, not being able to be there for them and give them the things they want, how would you feel inside?

Gregory: I'd feel like I'm failing.

Dr. McKay: Okay. You'd feel like you're failing. But what's the emotion? What you've said is kind of a thought, a conclusion. But what's the emotion that goes with that sense that you can't take care of them, you can't give them things?

Gregory: I guess I just feel like I'm not good enough. I'm ashamed of myself.

Dr. McKay: And, Gregory, does it seem like the same feeling that lurks behind the decision to buy that home entertainment center that Iris talked about? What would your feeling have been if you couldn't have gotten that for your family?

Gregory: I'd feel like I'm just not taking care of them. I want to get them something really nice, something to really enjoy.

Dr. McKay: And if you can't really take care of them? Is that the same feeling of shame?

Gregory: Yeah!

Now we're finding out something very important about Gregory. He too is struggling with shame. But Gregory copes with shame differently than Iris does. He wants to present a good face to the world. He wants to look good to his in-laws. He wants to be generous and caring toward his wife and children. He wants to have material signs of success around him, like the expensive home entertainment system he brought home for his family. If Iris gets her way, Gregory is going to feel painfully exposed as somehow incompetent and wrong. He's going to feel like he's failing—as a father, as a husband, and as a member of his extended family. In short, he'll feel that he's failing as a man.

Iris's shame is more specific. Iris is afraid of being exposed as someone who has not successfully made the transition to adulthood. She's afraid of appearing as a needy child in her parents' eyes. She fears being unable to manage the things adults are supposed to take care of, like giving her children a good education. And she's also afraid of her father concluding that she chose the wrong man—that her choice of Gregory as a husband will turn out to be just another example of Iris's poor judgment in her father's eyes.

Now it's time to work with Gregory and Iris to change the way they deal with money. To achieve this, we're going to have to validate the experience of shame that each of them struggles with. And we're going to have to find a way for them to make decisions about money that support both Iris and Gregory's basic values about what it means to be a good human being.

Dr. McKay: So, Gregory and Iris, I think we're finding out some important things about what really underlies this struggle. Gregory, for you it's so important to be generous—to take care of people, to take care of your family. It's important to get people something of value that will last. And it feels like, if you don't do that, you're a failure—you're doing things wrong. You're letting people down. And, Iris, on your side, it's really important to be financially self-sufficient, particularly in the eyes of your father. And to make sure that your kids get the kind of education that was central in your life. And if you don't do that, you feel like a failure. You feel like you're not doing things right.

So each of you is struggling with this sense of shame. But you each have very different ideas about what's right and how to avoid those feelings of shame.

So I want to ask you, what do you think needs to change in this family about money, so that each of you can feel good about yourselves?

Iris: Well, one thing that would help me a lot—and maybe it would help us a lot—is if decisions about big purchases could be made together instead of Gregory just making them on his own, without consulting me. I really think that we should talk about big purchases, maybe anything over $200 or so.

Dr. McKay: Does that include taking your folks or other people out to dinner, or buying presents?

Iris: I'd like it to. I'd feel more comfortable if we have a game plan before we go out to a big dinner. And maybe if Gregory says to me, "Look, it's really important to me tonight to treat," maybe we could choose a slightly less expensive restaurant, or maybe we could have a big dinner party at home.

Dr. McKay: So you'd like to make conscious, collaborative decisions about how to spend money.

Iris: I think we need to! You know, we're at the beginning stages of our life together as a family.

Dr. McKay: What about Gregory's gifts to his clients, when he sells a home? You were concerned about that. What do you want to do about that?

Iris: When I think about it, I really understand, Gregory, that it's all about impressions in your business. It's really important. I mean, that's how we first met, when I was doing the flower arrangements for the houses you were showing. And I liked that in you, that you really thought about those things, and you noticed them, and you noticed that people noticed them. But the present that you give people after they buy a house—that isn't going to help your business, really; and it's not going to help our family.

Dr. McKay: So, Iris, what would feel good to you is to make decisions together, as partners, about any significant expenditures.

Iris: Yeah. And now that I kind of understand more about where this is coming from with Gregory, I'll try to be sensitive to his needs.

Gregory: If I listened to Iris, in terms of buying a television, we'd have a thirteen-inch black-and-white TV with rabbit ears instead of a nice entertainment center. She'd just go out and do everything on the cheap!

Iris: Okay, Gregory. But if we're *talking* about purchases before we make them, then that won't happen, because we'll reach some kind of compromise, right?

Gregory: I guess so.

Dr. McKay: Let me break in here. So, just to make sure I understand where your feelings are, Iris. You want to make sure that there's money for the children's education and that you're not in a position of having to go to your dad for money, because that's really humiliating for you.

Iris: It's horrible.

Dr. McKay: And you want to make decisions about purchases together, so you can avoid those kinds of situations.

Iris: And to have a plan before we go out to dinner with the family.

Dr. McKay: Now, Gregory, what about you? What do you think needs to change about how the two of you spend money, so that your needs are taken care of here?

Gregory: I'd like to think, for one, that when we do make a decision about a major purchase, it's between me and my wife, not me and my wife and my father-in-law.

Dr. McKay: So you don't want your father-in-law looking over your shoulder and deciding what's good for your family?

Gregory: I think Iris needs to think for herself.

Dr. McKay: So you'd like to have privacy about spending decisions.

Gregory: Well, I'd like this to be our marriage, and I'd like this stuff to stay within our marriage.

Dr. McKay: Now, Iris wants to make sure there's money for the children, for their education. She wants to not be worried about having to borrow from her dad or having to answer his questions about your financial situation. I know you want to make sure that you can be a generous person—to your children, to your wife, to your in-laws—and that you can buy the best products possible, things that really work and will last a long time. How are we going to make sure that those needs are met, at the same time that we're taking care of Iris's concern that she not have to go to her father for money, that she not have to answer to him, and that she can send all three children to Catholic school, which was an important part of *her* life.

Gregory: Well, maybe, for one, Iris could break out and get another job that has nothing to do with her dad. I mean, for God's sake, the old guy pays minimum wage. Iris can do better, with all that good Catholic school education.

Dr. McKay: That sounds like an idea that we really should examine, Gregory. But I'm still interested in how we can put together both of your needs—yours and Iris's—about how to spend money. You want to be generous, and Iris wants to have money to send the kids to Catholic school. You want to buy high-quality products that will last, and Iris wants to make sure she doesn't have to borrow money from her dad. And both of you feel ashamed and embarrassed when you can't do the things that are important to you. So, Gregory, what do you think is a way that you can change your spending patterns to reflect both your needs, yours and Iris's?

Gregory: I guess we can talk about what we're going to buy in advance. I guess we can do that. But she won't let me buy anything if we do that. Everything will be "el cheapo." I'll never be able to take anybody out to eat, I won't be able to buy decent presents for my clients—it'll just be scrimp, scrimp, scrimp! That's basically how it's going be.

Dr. McKay: So what you're saying, Gregory, is that you don't think that making decisions collaboratively with Iris will allow you to be the generous person you want to be. You're convinced that would mean living a very frugal life.

Gregory: Yeah! I think that's basically the problem. If I just go to her for everything, she's just going to say, "Don't do it. Do it on the cheap."

Iris: You know, Gregory, I really think we can work together on this. For a long time I've been wondering if there might be some business opportunities for us together, working together. The thing that we have always done with the flowers in the houses—that's really special, and maybe we could branch out. Maybe it's something we could provide for other real estate agents. Not in your immediate area, so they wouldn't be competing against you. But maybe it's a business idea. Maybe we could start making more money. Maybe you're right—maybe I should stop working for my dad, or start another business on the side. We could get my sister to help with the kids after school, so I could work with you a little bit more.

Gregory: Yeah, but the question is, could I take somebody out to dinner? Can I buy my clients anything to show my gratitude for trusting me with the sale? Where does it leave me?

Iris: What I'm saying is that all this is stuff we would decide together. And it wouldn't just be me controlling you and stopping you. It would be us deciding what makes sense. And I think we can do that.

Gregory: If Iris got out of this minimum-wage job with her father, that would be a big help. If she could get something that paid more, I think we could make ends meet better. And I guess I am willing to talk to her about how we spend money. I guess I just have to get used to having her tell me what she thinks. Maybe I won't agree with it. But I'm just going to, I guess, listen to what she thinks.

Dr. McKay: Gregory, are you going to try to listen? Or are you really committed to listening?

Gregory: What do you mean?

Dr. McKay: It isn't enough just to make a promise Iris wants to hear. For this relationship to work, you're going to have to be committed to that promise every single day.

Gregory: I don't want my marriage to fall apart. If we have to make money decisions jointly from now on—at least, when it comes to the big-ticket items—I'm going to give it my best shot.

Therapist's Overview

Those who claim that money is the root of all evil are certainly exaggerating. But only a little. Studies show that conflicts over money engender more arguments between couples than any other issue. That's because money has such extraordinary symbolic value in our culture.

For many people, money is synonymous with freedom. It means independence and choice. Any limitation or diminishing of what they can spend triggers a sharp sense of engulfment, of being controlled. Often, they react by spending more, to reassert autonomy. I'm in charge: see my new $700 camera?

For others, money means safety and security, and spending it feels dangerous. Even a small reduction in the bank account can trigger a sense of being vulnerable and exposed. There is a core fear of loss, a perception that everything is fragile and can be swept away, even one's relationships. And the only way to be truly safe is to have enough money to weather any catastrophe.

Money is also an emblem suggesting status. The ability to spend conspicuously tells the world that you are a person of importance and value. It says you are smart, competent, and successful. Not having money to spend often makes you feel just the opposite—like you're inadequate, inept, and a loser.

In our example case, Gregory's fear of shame powers his over-spending. Flamboyant generosity, the state-of-the-art home theater system, the philosophy of buying nothing but the best all speak to an underlying sense of unworthiness, which Gregory has learned to cover with lavish expenditures.

But while Gregory is masking his shame with big spending, the resulting money crunch exacerbates his wife's shame. She's embarrassed in front of her dad and feels like a bad parent because she can't afford to send her children to parochial school.

For some, money represents excitement. It's the access to good times and glitter, to fun people and exotic places. Not having money means being stuck in a dull, empty life. Lots of folks either compulsively spend or compulsively save in exchange for a few shining days free of the monotony.

For many people, money spells relief. Their bank accounts represent a dream of retirement, deliverance from toil, from having to say "Yes, sir" to the boss, from all the structures that control their time. Every dime they spend is irksome, because it puts off that day when they retire.

The symbolic power of money is never so obvious as with gifts. The more expensive the gift we receive, the more it says we are valued, loved, irreplaceable. So we sometimes seek the big diamond or the budget-killing restaurant because the gift proves our worth in the other person's eyes.

Because money is an icon for so many needs and fears, it's no wonder it becomes a battleground for couples. They struggle with colliding agendas. One spends money to cover shame, while the other saves it to ensure safety. One spends to avoid feelings of emptiness, while the other saves for a dream of freedom and deliverance. The stakes seem so high that partners often get locked into knee-jerk responses that blind them to powerful underlying fears.

To get unstuck, we suggest you put aside the specifics of your conflict and explore the deeper issues. To do this you can use the Couples Research Form that follows.

Couples Research Form

Issue/Conflict: _____

_____

Fears: *What does my partner fear might happen in regard to our financial situation?* _____

_____

Other feelings my partner has about money: _____

_____

History: *What are my partner's experiences from the past (this or other relationships or childhood experiences) that relate to saving and spending?* _____

_____

Assumptions: *What are my partner's beliefs about money—about what will happen in the future; about my motives, feelings, and intentions?* _____

_____

Perceived choices: *What options does my partner believe he or she has about the way we deal with our finances?* _____

_____

Needs: *What does my partner want and need in regard to the way we use, save, and spend money?* _____

_____

Adapted from *When Anger Hurts Your Relationship* by Kim Paleg, Ph.D., and Matthew McKay, Ph.D. Used by permission.

Action Plan #1: Fill Out the Couples Research Form

You can do this exercise with your partner if your partner is willing to participate. The exercise will still be useful if you do it alone. In that case, fill out the form twice, once with your own responses and once answering the questions from what you imagine to be your partner's point of view. Just trying to think about the issues from his or her perspective will give you valuable information.

Begin the process by working (alone or collaboratively) on a brief, neutral description of your problem with money. If you're working together, expect that you may have some difficulty with this, because you're likely to have different perceptions of the conflict. Here are some ideas to help you write a description that will feel fair and accurate to both of you.

One of you should begin by writing a one- or two-sentence description of the problem on a separate piece of paper. "We disagree about saving versus spending" is an example of a sentence that's direct and nonblaming. It is important to use nonjudgmental language.

Now have your partner read your description and rewrite it, if necessary. Make sure that the sentence you agree upon feels like an accurate description for both of you and is both neutral and precise. Continue the process, passing the draft back and forth, until you reach a mutually satisfactory statement of the problem. If you're working alone, make every effort to get inside your partner's head and express his or her point of view.

Now start the actual interview process. Flip a coin, if you want— but you'll both get a turn interviewing the other, as well as a turn expressing your own perceptions and feelings.

Starting with *fears*, ask your partner:

- What are you afraid would happen if we adopted (or continued) my way of spending money?
- Can you be more specific about what you fear would be the effect on our relationship, our future, our well-being as

individuals if we adopted (or continued) my way of spending money?

Going to the *other feelings* section, ask your partner:

- Do you have other feelings that come up around this issue?

In terms of *history*, ask your partner:

- What experiences from your past have influenced your attitudes or feelings about money?
- When you were growing up, did your family have conflicts or issues about money?
- Is there any event that we've experienced together that influenced your attitude or feelings about money?

Under *assumptions*, ask your partner the following questions:

- How do you look at our conflicts about money? What do you think is the cause?
- What do you believe are the psychological issues underlying our problems with money?
- What's your sense of what makes me use money the way I do?
- How do you think our money issues will affect us over time?

Under *perceived choices*, try one or more of these questions:

- What choices do we have with this issue?
- Are there any options open to us that might help us resolve this issue?
- Is there any compromise open to us regarding spending patterns and priorities?

Under *needs*, ask your partner:

- What do you need to see changed that would ease our conflict about money?
- If we spent money exactly the way you want, what would that look like?

Be certain, as you do the interview, to record the main responses your partner gives to every question. Don't correct, refute, judge, or even comment on anything he or she says. Consider yourself a neutral journalist just trying to get the facts.

Hearing and writing down what your partner says doesn't mean you have to agree with it. Your job right now is merely to understand it. If you're working alone, your job is to exert the greatest amount of empathy possible for your partner's point of view.

As soon as the interview is complete, reverse the process. The interviewer now becomes the interviewee and answers all the questions he or she just asked.

Here is an example showing how two of my clients—two people in their late forties who were contemplating living together—began to use the couples interview to get to the root of their conflicts over money:

Duane: What are you afraid would happen if we adopted (or continued) my way of spending money?

Julie: I couldn't stand living that way! I don't want to think about money as much as you think about it. I don't want to think about it at all!

Duane: Can you be more specific about what you're afraid would be the effect on our relationship, our future, our well-being as individuals if we adopted my way of spending money?

Julie: I don't want to find myself an old lady cutting out coupons every Sunday to save a couple of bucks. Or wearing out shoe leather so I won't have to pay for parking.

Duane: Do you have other feelings that come up around this issue?

Julie: I just don't want to have that impoverished flavor to my life. We both make good salaries. I don't want to live like I'm always afraid all the time.

Duane: What experiences from your past have influenced your attitudes or feelings about money?

Julie: All this penny-pinching I see you do reminds me of all my old Jewish relatives. It doesn't seem like a mentality that is relevant for you and me.

Duane: When you were growing up, did your family have conflicts or issues about money?

Julie: My mom was just like you. She and my dad had plenty of money, but she could never allow herself to enjoy it.

Duane: Is there any event that we've experienced together that influenced your attitude or feelings about money?

Julie: Well, that time you drove two hundred miles just to use that coupon at the batting cages when you could have taken your kids to the place nearby and just paid the twenty bucks. I mean, you spent more than that on gas! It really made me question whether this is a good idea, our moving in together.

Duane: How do you look at our conflicts about money? What do you think is the cause?

Julie: I guess our attitudes stem from the experiences we had in our own families. And those were so different! I guess because your parents were immigrants and my grandparents were the ones who were immigrants, we're one generation apart on those issues.

Duane: What's your sense of what makes me use money the way that I do?

Julie: I think it has something to do with your fear of loss. Maybe because your wife left you the way she did, or maybe it's from a fear of loss that comes from earlier on in your life. Maybe you felt emotionally abandoned by your parents, and being supercareful with money is a way of feeling safe.

Duane: Are there any options open to us that might help us resolve this issue?

Julie: We could keep our money separate. That might help both of us feel safe from having our worst fears aggravated by the way the other one spends money (or, in your case, doesn't spend money).

Duane: Is there any compromise open to us regarding spending patterns and priorities?

Julie: I'd like it if you could relax more about spending. And I'd be more than willing to listen and respond to you when some of your abandonment fears get activated by money issues.

Duane: What are your needs in this issue?

Julie: I need to feel like I don't have to think about money all the time, or feel guilty if I'm ordering something expensive from the menu. I need to feel that you're going to show me you love me in everything you do, including the way you spend money on me.

Duane: If we spent money exactly the way you want, what would that look like?

Julie: We'd be focusing on having fun together rather than on how much we're spending. We'd live within our means—which means we'd be living pretty well.

When you've completed your interview, even if you're working alone, you'll have collected a treasure trove of useful information, with new insights about your partner's and perhaps your own feelings and needs. This resource can serve as the foundation for a new era of respect between you, for empathy instead of blame, and a refined understanding of your own feelings.

Action Plan #2: The Compromise

Couple conflicts must be solved together. You need to work collaboratively toward a compromise that makes sense to both of you. Let go right now of the hope that your needs will prevail, that you'll win this one. Compromise grows from a commitment to finding solutions that incorporate both your needs.

There are six basic structures for compromise:

1. My way this time, your way next time.
2. My way when I'm doing it, your way when you're doing it. (Or, "My way in this situation, your way in that situation.")
3. Split the difference.
4. Part of what I want with part of what you want.
5. If you do _____ for me, I'll do _____ for you.
6. Try it my way for a week (a month, a year). If you don't like it, we can go back to the old way.

Each of you should now sit down and write your own proposed compromise to your money conflict. Structure your compromise in one of the above six ways. Remember, the compromise must offer something for each of you; it must provide for some (but probably not all) of your needs. Make your proposal simple and explicit.

The next step is to exchange what you've written. If you can both agree to one of the two proposals, make specific plans to carry it out. If not, discuss the problems with each proposal, and write two new ones. Stick with the process until you've agreed on a compromise plan.

If you're working without your partner's input, put together your own list of six possible compromises. You can use these as the basis for discussion the next time the issue comes up for you.

7

Children

Am I Ready for This?

Paul and Enid were an East Coast couple who came to see me while Paul was on sabbatical in California. In the seventeen years they'd been together, they'd worked through a number of painful issues, mostly on their own. Enid was just twenty-one when they got married and was at the tail end of an eating disorder that Paul didn't fully understand until after they'd said, "I do." Although Paul, twelve years older than his wife, was and continued to be very much in love with her, he traveled a lot in his work and sometimes enjoyed the favors of other women. This wasn't an issue until Enid found out about it. It took them a couple of years to sort out the hurt and betrayal she felt.

By the time they came to see me, though, Paul and Enid had achieved an admirable level of happiness in their marriage. They loved and valued the time they spent together. They were capable, too, of spending time apart. They had good sex. They laughed a lot. They traveled and ate together with great enjoyment. They had lots of friends but were each other's best friend.

But as Enid got closer to turning forty, Paul began to get in touch with a deeply held desire to have children. He was the American-born child of a Mexican family that had prospered in the United States with a car-washing franchise. Both Paul and his brother had multiple advanced degrees. But Paul's brother was gay. When their father passed away, Paul began to realize that the burden was completely on him to carry on the family name. He wanted to have a child to whom he could teach Spanish. Enid, who was born in France, pointed out that Paul himself had never been fluent in Spanish, as his family was bent on assimilation. But Paul still harbored an ideal of cultural continuity that would be carried on through his child.

Enid was an elegant and gracious woman who had perfected the art of being Paul's wife. In the past few years, she had also come into her own, plugging away at a career as a painter that had finally begun, against all odds, to pay off. Her work was being shown in galleries both in New York and Paris. One of the glossy architectural magazines had just published an article that featured one of Enid's canvasses in the background. Determined since adolescence to make it as an artist, Enid felt that she was finally on her way.

When Paul first brought up the issue of having a baby, Enid suggested that perhaps they could get a puppy. They did that, and it was diverting enough for the first year. They both loved their dog. But then Paul started having disturbing dreams—dreams about children crying, dreams about his dead father.

Enid was worried that having children would wreck both her career and her marriage. She felt that Paul didn't understand the extent to which he himself was the baby in their relationship—he took for granted all the nurturing Enid gave him, paving his way at every step to make sure his life went smoothly. Paul had even been jealous of time she spent seeing after the puppy's needs. How would he cope with all the motherly attention required by a baby? And how could Enid just blithely abandon her career, when suddenly, for the first time in her life, she was feeling so successful on her own? She painted in oils, which her OB/GYN had said might be toxic during pregnancy; and the fumes were likely to make her feel too sick to work anyway, at least during her first trimester.

She worried about the wear and tear on her body that having a baby would cause, to say nothing of sleep deprivation. Enid knew that her beauty and relative youthfulness were a big part of her attractiveness to Paul. She also knew about his tendency to stray. She was not at all confident that Paul would still love her with swollen ankles and a pregnant belly, or in the slow aftermath while she tried to care for their baby and get back into shape.

Paul, in desperation, suggested a trial separation. Enid wondered whether this meant that he had already picked out someone else to replace her—someone who would be willing to have his child.

Paul and Enid's Commitment Dialogue

Dr. McKay: Paul, you and Enid have had some serious issues come up in the last few months. From your point of view, what do you hope to gain from therapy right now?

Paul: This issue about whether we're going to have a child together has assumed a kind of urgency for me lately. Those dreams that I mentioned to you are occurring with more frequency.

Dr. McKay: The dreams about your father?

Paul: Yes, and the dream of the child crying. I feel that this is a tremendously important thing for me to do in my life. And I realize that if I don't do this now, it's something that could pass me by.

Dr. McKay: So your sense is that having a child is really important to you right now. And you feel that if you don't act soon, it might never happen; you might lose this chance.

Paul: Some things in life happen whether you put work into them or not, and other things in life require action. They require you to be decisive. This is something very important for me.

Dr. McKay: And if you don't have a child, what does that mean?

Paul: I will have failed.

Dr. McKay: You will have failed? Failed in what way?

Paul: I will have failed my family. Even at the most essential biological level, this is what we are here to do beyond all else—beyond all the details, the work we make for ourselves on this earth. Underneath it all, our job is to reproduce.

Dr. McKay: Enid, when you're listening to Paul talk about the importance for him of having a child, what happens inside you?

Enid: You know, doctor, I really feel what Paul is saying. I feel how important it is for him. But I also know Paul. And there's something about this urgency that I recognize. I recognize it as part of a greater need, part of a larger picture of who Paul has always been for as long as I've known him.

Dr. McKay: Part of a greater need—what is that need, Enid?

Enid: It takes different forms. For a while, early on in our relationship, it had to do with his career and obtaining a tenure-track position. And once he had that, he moved on to the next thing, and it had to do with establishing himself in his field in a certain way. And then it was establishing himself on campus as a spokesman. He had a following of students, often attractive female students, who simply worshipped him. He has been a great spokesman, a great mentor for many young people. He has articulated many of their longings and he's been a hero to many—sometimes too much of a hero, I think. I hesitate to bring this up, but there have been times when one or another of those young women—

Paul: Do we have to get into this now? These things are in the past. They're over now, Enid. You know that. I've sworn to you.

Enid: I know they're over, Paul. But, still, they are part of the story. You're someone who's always putting things into their historical context. I think Dr. McKay needs to hear the context of your longing for a child.

Dr. McKay: So, Enid, what you're describing to me is that Paul has had some sort of need that drove him to establish himself, that drove him to be an important person in the campus community, drove him to cultivate a following of appreciative students who looked to him as a mentor and spokesman. How do you see that need relating to what's happening today, in terms of the need to have a child?

Enid: I can't help questioning the confluence of events here. We put the infidelities behind us. And I trust Paul; I know he won't do that again. But his father died recently, and suddenly now there is this urgency Paul feels to have a child, to carry on his family name. And I can't help wondering, is it taking the place of the infidelities?

Dr. McKay: So what is this need that lies behind the drive to succeed academically, the drive to be an important person to the student community, the drive perhaps to connect in intimate ways with other people? Do you know what that is?

Enid: I think it's all of what makes Paul who he is. He is a driven person. He's a tremendously ambitious person. And he's a very successful man. I think now this is simply part of the picture, his picture that he has of what it means to have a successful life.

Dr. McKay: Paul, this drive Enid sees in you—in your need to have a child, to build your career and even perhaps to connect to people outside of your marriage—this drive she sees as all part of one sort of basic impulse. Do you know what she's talking about?

Paul: Yes, I'm sure I do. I think Enid knows me well and has had the opportunity to watch me carefully through the years, to experience many of these things with me. And it's part of the drive to become the best version of myself I can—to fulfill my promise, my destiny.

Dr. McKay: Paul, let me ask you something. If you and Enid were not to have a child, what do you think you'd feel? What would life feel like to you?

Paul: It would feel like it was all for nothing. I would feel a great sense of nothingness.

Dr. McKay: Nothingness. Tell me more about that. What is that nothingness? You and Enid—for some reason you don't have a child. We're imagining a future where you are living together and there is no child that's part of your life. That nothingness—what is it like? What does it feel like, look like?

Paul: It feels so unacceptable to me. It feels like a mistake, as if somehow we had taken the wrong turn, and we had gotten off the road we were supposed to be on.

Dr. McKay: So that's one way of thinking about it—that you've somehow gotten diverted from the true path you should have taken. But describe the feeling of that nothingness, of not having that child, of that life with Enid but no child. What does that feel like?

Paul: Terrible emptiness! Loss. A sense of no meaning, of futility. This striving, the work, the focus, the struggle—what is it for? It's supposed to be for this very basic human need, this need of all organic life to reproduce.

Dr. McKay: Now, Enid has talked about her sense that your need to have a child is somehow connected to needs you've had in the past: the need to build a career, the need to have a prominent place in the campus community, the need on occasion to connect intimately with people outside the marriage. Enid has talked about her sense that those needs are all one and the same. Do you see it that way, or does your need to have a child feel different to you?

Paul: I see all of these other things as being only to serve that final goal of having a child. Not only having a child, but raising a child, and having that child be a bridge to the future.

Dr. McKay: So, for you, Paul, having a child means having the world make sense.

Paul: It's the living articulation of the connection that Enid and I have. It's the embodiment of our love, of what we've striven for over the years, of what we've worked for. What meaning does it have without a child—if it's just the two of us and it dies with the two of us?

We're now learning from Paul that the need to have a child grows strongly from a need to have meaning, a need to have a central focus in his life. Enid suggests to us that Paul has been looking for this for a long time. He's looked for it in his career, he's looked for it on campus, he's looked for it in other sexual relationships. That need is surfacing again, now recast as a focus on having children. But whether that need is longstanding and has appeared in other guises before, or is something that's unique and specific at this moment in Paul's life, the fact remains that Paul is very strongly convinced that his life will not feel fulfilled—and that the emptiness will continue—unless he and Enid find a way to have a child together.

Dr. McKay: Enid, let me ask you a question. If you and Paul were to have a child, and if you, in the next year or two, were to have this very big change in the way you live together, what do you see about your life and your relationship to Paul that might change, that might be different?

Enid: Having a child would be a major revolution, not only to me and Paul but to my career. To my body. To everything—every aspect of my life would change. I work in oils, Dr. McKay. If I were pregnant, I couldn't work; I couldn't work the way I do. The fumes from the turpentine, from the paints, would be harmful. I would be harming my child.

Dr. McKay: So while you were pregnant, you would have to be careful—

Enid: I smoke! I couldn't smoke and be pregnant. I would have to change so much. And being pregnant—swelling and feeling ill. Yes, all of those things—I could manage it. Women have always managed it. But I'm not sure that Paul is really thinking about the practical aspects of this undertaking. He is looking at the heroic picture—the large, heroic, abstract picture. But, when it comes to the actual business of being pregnant and having to make changes, having to make sacrifices, it's not Paul who will be making these changes and sacrifices. It would be me.

Dr. McKay: So what would happen to your relationship with Paul if you had a child—as your body changed during pregnancy and after giving birth, if you looked different to Paul? What do you think would happen?

Enid: There's no doubt that I would look different to Paul—and, I don't know! Judging from the past, I would have many fears. Many fears.

Dr. McKay: What would you be afraid of?

Enid: I'm quite a bit younger than Paul, as I think you know. And I think he's always been drawn to my youth, and he's been attracted to me. I'm not very sure that I would continue to be attractive to Paul. Perhaps he would look elsewhere.

Dr. McKay: You're afraid of losing him?

Enid: Yes, I would be afraid of losing him.

Dr. McKay: So having a child, for you, Enid, feels as if it would be putting this marriage at risk.

Enid: Absolutely. Because I don't think Paul is being realistic. I don't think he's thinking about the reality of what pregnancy and a child would mean for us.

Dr. McKay: So your appearance might change—

Enid: It would definitely change!

Dr. McKay: What else would change?

Enid: My very identity would change. You know, Paul doesn't realize, I think, the extent to which I care for him, I nurture him. I, of course, try to keep it all as transparent as possible. But even when we got the dog, and I spent lots of time training it, taking care of it, Paul was jealous, and it was difficult for him. I know it was! He suffered. I don't want Paul to suffer. I don't want him to fulfill this dream only to find that it makes him hurt.

Dr. McKay: And if you were preoccupied with a child, as sometimes you were focused on the dog, what would happen then? What do you think would change in your relationship to Paul?

Enid: I would be taking care of our child. And Paul . . . he would perhaps look for someone to take care of him. He's a man who is used to being taken care of.

Dr. McKay: Your fear is that you wouldn't have time to take care of him, and as a result he would turn his attention away from you and away from this family.

Enid: From everything that I understand, a child takes a great deal of time.

Paul: Enid, I think you misjudge me! I understand what it is to have a child. And I would be there with you. I would be taking care of our child with you. It's nonsense to think that this is all an abstraction for me. I am a man of the world. I understand what it means to have a baby.

Enid: I don't think there's room for me to take care of two people in this relationship.

Paul: Honestly, I think perhaps you've forgotten the extent to which I've taken care of you. What has made your career possible, after all? Who has made that career possible?

Enid: Yes, it's true, Paul. I would be the first to admit, the first to give you credit: you've made it possible for me to live as an artist. But you also must acknowledge that whenever you have a need, I am there for you. You come first. You've always come first. And if we were to have a child, that would not be the case any more.

Dr. McKay: So, Enid, the feeling that you have is that while Paul very much desires to have a child, to have someone to carry on his line, to be a central focus of meaning in his life, if you were to bear him that child, it would somehow unravel your relationship. You would lose Paul.

Enid: I would lose so much! I would lose Paul. I would lose my art. I would lose myself!

Dr. McKay: Let me explore that with you. You feel you would lose Paul and you would also lose your art and yourself. What are you thinking of when you say that?

Enid: I don't see how I could paint the way I paint, take care of Paul, and have a child. There simply wouldn't be emotional space to do all of that.

Dr. McKay: You talked about not being able to paint while you were pregnant. But you're also saying that you might lose your career, you might lose your art, if you were a new mother and having to focus on a child.

Enid: It's going so well now. I just had a show in Germany. I sold many paintings there. It's an important time in my career, a sort of fruition. To stop now would be a disaster for me.

Dr. McKay: So you might really lose momentum, and lose the time you need to produce your art. You also said you would lose yourself. What do you mean?

Enid: It's my sense of what justifies my being alive. What I create, what I'm able to do—it's very much what Paul said about his work. I, too, feel that I have to justify my existence, fulfill the gift I have to the greatest extent I can.

Enid has two core fears that are influencing her reaction to Paul and his quest to start a family. The first fear is abandonment—that Paul will lose his sexual interest in her as her body changes with pregnancy and the effects of childbearing. She fears that as she focuses on the needs of a child and her parenting begins to compete with Paul's need for her nurturance and attention, Paul will begin to slip away. He will not be able to tolerate Enid as a parent and will seek others who can nurture him in the way she did before having a child.

The second core fear for Enid is engulfment. Her career as an artist is beginning to catch fire. Her recent show has been very successful. Her commitment to art is an important part of her self-

identity. She fears that motherhood will so compete with her life as an artist that she will have to choose one or the other. And if she chooses motherhood, she will lose her reason for being.

Dr. McKay: Paul and Enid, there are some really important needs and fears that are lying behind the struggle we're talking about. On the one hand, Paul, you need to feel a sense of meaning and purpose and focus; and, without that, you fear what you call emptiness—a sense of yearning, a sense of absence. But for you, Enid, there are different needs—the need to hold on to this relationship, which you feel would be threatened if you were to have a child; and the fear that you might lose yourself, that you might lose your focus and momentum as an artist and your sense of who you really are.

Each of you has needs and fears that are equally important, that have equal weight in this relationship. We need to begin with that basic idea, that the needs and fears of each of you have equal importance, equal validity. I want to ask you how as partners you might respond to these very important needs and these very important fears as you struggle with this decision about having a child.

Paul: First, I would like to reassure Enid that it would be the opposite of what she fears. Having a child would cement our bond, for me—even more than it is cemented in my heart already.

Dr. McKay: But she's saying that she's afraid you'll lose interest. That as her body changes, you'll lose interest. As she becomes preoccupied with parenting, that you'll feel like you're not getting enough nourishment and support and you'll drift away.

Paul: But Enid needs to understand that my bond to her is far deeper than the bond of our bodies and the bond of sexual attraction. It's love that I feel for her, for who she is inside!

Enid: Paul, I believe that you believe the words you're saying. I do! I know you're saying them from your heart with complete sincerity. But I also feel that sometimes you, like everyone else, don't truly understand your own reactions. You can't anticipate them. I know you, Paul!

Dr. McKay: So you're saying that reassurance is not really making you feel safer, not making you feel confident that this relationship could survive a child.

Enid: I think there are so many unknowns. This whole idea of the child—it's a tremendous thing for the child to live up to. What if the child is a difficult child? What if it's a homely child?

Dr. McKay: What do you need from Paul so that you would feel confident that this relationship will truly last?

Enid: I need to know that Paul is committed to our marriage—our marriage with a child or our marriage without a child. I don't want our marriage to hinge on first having a child and then on my being able to recover after pregnancy and be attractive to Paul once again.

Dr. McKay: Do you need more than words from Paul?

Enid: I don't know what I can get. There's no contract he can sign. These things come with no guarantee. Children come with no guarantee. What if we had a child that had something wrong with it, God forbid?

Dr. McKay: What about your fear that a child, and being a parent, would really get in the way of your life as an artist?

Paul: If I could say something. We are in a position so that I could hire help for you. You would be able to paint every day. And perhaps, while you are pregnant, you could paint in acrylics instead of oils. I know it would not be your ideal; but, still, it would mean you could continue to paint.

Dr. McKay: You're saying, Paul, that there's a way to get the help and support necessary for Enid to continue being an artist.

Paul: Absolutely. And I completely support her career. I would feel like a criminal stopping her from doing what she does so well.

Dr. McKay: Enid, what happens for you—to that fear that you'll lose your center, your artistic core—when Paul talks about setting up a life where you can get the help necessary to continue?

Enid: It's somewhat reassuring. I'm glad to hear these words. But, again, I wonder—are they only words? How would they translate into reality? I just feel there are so many imponderables, so many things we can't know.

Dr. McKay: There's a sense I have that you're unconvinced that Paul's emptiness would be satisfied very long by having a child—that he might again feel that need, that hunger, for something to fill that place in him. That was part of his drive to be an academic, part of his drive to be an important person on campus, part of his drive to connect to other people. And you're not sure that that won't reemerge.

Enid: I think Paul needs to find a way to fill this feeling of emptiness from within himself, and not to keep looking for it in something outside himself. Otherwise it will never be filled. It's not something that can be filled by something from the outside—not by me, not by a child, not by a love affair.

Dr. McKay: Suppose the two of you had a child, and Paul again found himself, months or years down the line, struggling with that empty feeling. What would you need Paul to do so that you would know that he was still committed to the relationship, and you were still together, and you were not in any risk of losing him?

Enid: Not to sneak off and do something to fill his emptiness, but to talk to me.

Dr. McKay: You would need him to tell you what's going on.

Enid: Absolutely. Even more so if we had a child. I would need to know.

Dr. McKay: So what Enid is saying to you, Paul, is that she's not going to feel safe until she knows that if you find yourself disconnecting, find yourself beginning to focus on other people, find yourself beginning to hunger and yearn for something, that you will come to Enid with those feelings rather than act on them and somehow run away from this relationship.

Paul: I can understand that she would want that, and I would try to do that. That would seem the right thing to do.

Therapist's Overview

Perhaps no couple issue is more charged than the question of whether to have a baby. For some people, the thought of an eighteen-year commitment to raising a child sets off full-blown panic. To them, children form the bars on a trapped, unhappy existence. They fear being engulfed by a child's needs, by years of financial and emotional giving.

Enid, in our case example, struggles with this fear. A child, she expects, will suffocate her creative life.

While engulfment is often a factor in resistance to having children, any of the other key fears can exert an influence. Enid, for instance, is also afraid that childbearing will change her attractiveness to Paul. Perhaps worse, she imagines that Paul will resent the time she'll devote to parenting and ultimately abandon her.

The fear of emptiness can also trigger conflicts about having children. Paul hopes a child will fill some of the empty places inside him. But some people have the opposite reaction. They fear that children will prevent them from seeking the stimulation and excitement needed to mask their emptiness. Or that the endless hours spent caring for a baby will leave them feeling disconnected and alone.

The fear of shame can play a significant role in the baby debate. Some people fear they won't be good parents. They may have grown up with a lot of anger or abuse, and envision a horrifying future in which they could inflict the same damage. "Inside everyone who's been abused is an abuser," a client of mine once confided. "I don't trust myself with a child."

If your relationship gets stuck on the issue of whether to have children, consider the possibility that one or both of you may be struggling with a key underlying fear. The answer is to put aside, temporarily, the question of children and look a little deeper. We suggest using the Couples Research Form that follows to explore some critical needs and fears each of you may bring to the issue.

Couples Research Form

Issue/Conflict: _____

_____

Fears: *What does my partner fear might happen?* _____

_____

Other feelings my partner has about this issue: _____

_____

History: *What are my partner's experiences from the past (this or other relationships or childhood experiences) that relate to this issue?* _____

_____

Assumptions: *What are my partner's beliefs about this issue — about what will happen in the future; about my motives, feelings, and intentions?* _____

Perceived choices: *What options does my partner believe he or she has regarding this issue?* _____

_____

Needs: *What does my partner want and need?* _____

_____

Adapted from *When Anger Hurts Your Relationship* by Kim Paleg, Ph.D., and Matthew McKay, Ph.D. Used by permission.

Action Plan #1: Fill Out the Couples Research Form

You can do this exercise by yourself, even if your partner is unwilling to participate in the process. In that case, you will fill out the form twice—once for yourself and once for your partner, doing the best you can to capture his or her perceptions, memories, and point of view.

Make two copies of the form. Now, working together or alone, write a brief, neutral description of your conflicts over the issue of having children. You may have some difficulty with this if you discover that each of you has a very different perception of the problem. Here are a few suggestions (if you're working together) for writing a description that will feel fair and accurate for both of you.

Write a one- or two-sentence description of the conflict on a separate piece of paper. "One of us wants to start a family, the other doesn't" is an example of a description that's simple and nonblaming. It is important to use language that is as nonjudgmental as possible.

Now let your partner read your description and rewrite it, if necessary, to incorporate his or her point of view. Whether you're working together or alone, make a real effort to be neutral and accurate. Continue the process, passing the draft back and forth, until you arrive at a statement of the conflict that's acceptable to both of you (or that seems like a fair description to you if you're working by yourself).

At this point you should begin the actual interview process. It doesn't matter which of you goes first; you'll each get a turn interviewing and being interviewed. If you're working by yourself, role-play your partner in coming up with answers that you honestly believe reflect his or her point of view.

Starting with *fears*, ask your partner:

- What are you afraid will happen if I got my way on this issue?
- What are you afraid will happen if we can't resolve this issue?

- Do you have any worries about what might happen if you got your way on this issue?

Going to the *other feelings* section, ask your partner:

- Do you have other feelings that come up around either having or not having a child?
- What feelings would you have if we finally decided we would—or wouldn't—have a child?
- What's the most difficult feeling that comes up for you around this issue?

In terms of *history*, ask your partner:

- What experiences have you had that made you want (or not want) children?
- What did you observe in your family that influenced your feelings about this issue?
- Is there anything about our experiences as a couple that influences your feelings about this issue?

Under *assumptions*, ask your partner some or all of the following questions:

- How do you see our conflict over having kids?
- What's the part of your point of view that didn't get included in our neutral description?
- What's your sense of what makes me feel the way I do about this issue?
- How do you think we'll deal with this conflict in the future?

Under *perceived choices*, try one or more of these questions:

- What choices do we have with this issue?
- Are there any options open to us that might help us resolve this conflict?

- Is any compromise available to us in terms of timing, degree of involvement in parenting, work responsibilities, lifestyle, etc.?

Under *needs*, ask your partner:

- What are your needs in this issue?
- What's the most important thing you need in relation to our conflict about having children?
- If things were exactly the way you wanted them, what would that situation look like?

Make sure that, as you do the interview, you've written down the main responses your partner gave to every question. Don't correct, judge, try to refute, or comment on anything he or she says. Just pretend you're a journalist trying to get the facts. You don't have to agree with everything your partner says; for now you just need to understand it.

As soon as the interview is complete, reverse the process. The interviewer becomes the interviewee and answers all the questions he or she just asked.

Here's an example showing how two of my clients—each of whom had children in a previous marriage—used the Couples Research Form to help them get a handle on their conflict over a stepparenting issue. Melanie and Brian were committed to each other, but Brian was very hesitant about becoming a stepfather to Melanie's young son. They adapted the form slightly, substituting questions about stepparenting for those having to do with whether or not to have a child together.

Melanie: What are you afraid will happen if I get my way on this issue and you become part of this family?

Brian: I'm worried I'll be spending all my spare time taking care of Joey.

Melanie: What are you afraid will happen if we can't resolve this issue?

Brian: I'm afraid of losing you.

Melanie: Do you have any worries about what might happen if you got your way on this issue?

Brian: I worry about you feeling overburdened, because you think I'm not doing my share. I worry about you feeling unhappy, or that you've made a mistake in choosing to be with me.

Melanie: Do you have other feelings that come up around either being or not being a stepparent?

Brian: I worry that I'm not naturally very good with young children. I don't feel a lot of confidence in relating to them. And I'm also worried about having such a young child at this late stage, when I've just finally gotten my own son out of the house and launched in his own life.

Melanie: What experiences have you had that made you want (or not want) to have more children?

Brian: I sort of feel that I've paid my dues already in raising my son. I never even considered, before I met you, the idea of helping to raise someone else's child.

Melanie: What did you observe in your family that influenced your feelings about this issue?

Brian: My parents weren't very affectionate or demonstrative people. I think it makes me feel like I don't know the language when it comes to being a parent to a very young child.

Melanie: Is there anything about our experiences as a couple that influences your feelings about this issue?

Brian: I really like and appreciate the way you are with Joey. I've actually felt that I've learned a lot from you in watching you parent him. I'm also really glad that his father plays an active role in Joey's life. I don't think I'd be a good choice as the main father for Joey at this stage in my life. I just don't know that I'd be up to the job.

Melanie: What's the part of your point of view that didn't get included in our neutral description?

Brian: My own feelings of inadequacy vis-à-vis parenting.

Melanie: What's your sense of what makes me feel the way I do about this issue?

Brian: I see your optimism at work. You want me to step up to the plate and be a great stepfather for Joey and to love him as much as I love you. And wanting it, for you, is almost the same as having it be real.

Melanie: What choices do we have with this issue?

Brian: Because I think we're both agreed we want to be together, I think our only choice is to find a way to make it work for both of us.

Melanie: Is any compromise available to us in terms of timing, degree of involvement in parenting, work responsibilities, lifestyle, etc.?

Brian: I think the more we can make sure the two of us have some time alone every week, the easier it will be for me to adjust to the times I'll spend with you and Joey as a family.

Melanie: What's the most important thing you need in relation to our conflict about the role you'll play in Joey's life?

Brian: I think it will help me a lot if we can work out some schedules and coordinate things so Joey's father does his fair share, both in terms of time and money. I want it to be clear to him that he's still Joey's main guy, even though I'll certainly be very involved.

The Couples Research Form can yield a huge amount of information, giving you new insights about your partner's and perhaps your own feelings and needs (even if you've done this exercise alone). Building respect for each other's needs, desires, and emotions will help you face conflicts with empathy rather than blame.

Action Plan #2: Shared Thoughts

Carve out some time—an hour or so should do it—to write down your thoughts on the following topics. You can do this exercise alone or with your partner.

1. Think for a moment about your partner's key needs and fears regarding the issue of having children. Is there anything *you* could do to allay those fears or, in part, provide for those needs (short of agreeing to your partner's preference in regard to having children)?

2. What if you agreed to have (or not have) children as your partner wishes? What would you need from him or her to possibly make this okay for you?

3. Imagine yourself five, and then ten, years from now. You've deferred to your partner's wishes and had (or not had) children. What does your life look like? What does your relationship feel like? What's the best thing about this life? What's the worst thing about it?

4. Imagine yourself five years from now. Your partner has gone along with your wishes regarding having children. What emotional impact might this have had on him or her? On the relationship? What's the best thing about your life together? What's the worst thing about it?

If your partner has done this exercise with you, exchange what you've written. After reading your partner's reactions, talk over what you've learned about each other and the issue. Be gentle and open. Appreciate the needs and fears that influence each of you.

8

Sex

What Happened to It?

Although they were both in their late forties, Bill and Emma had the look of people completely surprised by middle age, as if they'd gone to bed one night as young people and woken up the next morning worn, wrinkled, and filled with the sense that all their hopes and dreams had passed them by.

Bill was a jazz guitarist perpetually on the edge of his big break. He'd cut a few sample CDs and even opened a couple of shows for big-name musicians. But the groups he played with over the years always broke up. Early on in his career the members of his band dropped out to go back to school or to get married. Later his sax player landed in the hospital with lung cancer. His lead singer was in and out of detox programs so often there was no relying on him. But Bill soldiered on, sitting in at clubs when he got the chance, continuing to send his now very outdated CD to jazz station disk jockeys. He'd worked a regular full-time job for years as a sales clerk in a music store, watching the parade of younger, hipper clerks come and go with their changing display of rebellious fashion statements, from Mohawks to dreadlocks to faces so pierced Bill wondered they didn't spring leaks when they drank water.

He prided himself on staying fit and shunning the cigarettes and substance abuse that had brought so many of his buddies down. So it came as a horrible surprise to him, standing on a ladder one day to reach a box of drum keys, to overhear two of the thirty-something workers laughing about someone they referred to as "the geezer." Bill was just on the verge of poking his head down to ask them who they were talking about when he realized they were talking about him.

Emma and Bill had met at the chain restaurant where Emma worked as a waitress. Emma had been really pretty when she was younger, and she was still very striking. It pained her now to be, as she termed it, "invisible." She complained that men didn't even notice her at the restaurant any more. Her work was gruelingly hard on her body, and even harder on her spirit.

Emma had always thought she'd grow up and live happily ever after, surrounded by a houseful of cheerful kids and a man who made it all worthwhile. But the right guy had just never come along, and Emma's dreams about going back to school and getting a college degree never amounted to anything more than a collection of unrelated course credits at the local junior college.

She kept lowering the bar for Prince Charming until Bill shuffled into the restaurant one day and said, "What's up, doll?" From then on, she'd worked hard on constructing a fantasy of everything Bill could be for her, if he'd just let her take him in hand. She saw what she wanted to see in Bill—and he was happy enough to be on the receiving end of her romantic projection. He was tickled by all the attention and how Emma seemed to light up when she was in his company.

They were both rejuvenated by the first, wild six months of their relationship. The sex was the best part. They made love everywhere and anywhere; they couldn't believe they'd been trucking along all this time without each other.

And then, responding to Emma's irrefutable logic that they'd have even more opportunity to make love if they moved in together—and could save money, too—Bill moved out of his studio apartment downtown into Emma's one-bedroom house in the suburbs.

It was all downhill from there. Emma was suddenly making all the advances, and Bill just wasn't responding. She wept that it had gotten to the point where he seemed willing to go to any lengths to avoid having sex with her. She'd come home from her job to find him already asleep, or else he'd come home so late that she just couldn't wait up for him any longer. He'd have a stomachache or bad dreams or just a bad day. The more Bill withdrew from closeness, the more desperate Emma was to have it. Sex had been the glue that held their relationship together. And now it was as if that glue had just dried up and flaked away, and everything was falling to pieces. Bill had already started looking at apartments when Emma made an appointment for both of them to come see me.

Bill and Emma's Commitment Dialogue

Dr. McKay: Bill, when Emma makes it clear to you that she's interested in getting close, in connecting sexually, what happens inside you?

Bill: You know, spontaneity is the whole thing in the kind of music I play, in jazz. One person plays for a while, and then someone else joins in. And then maybe two of you are playing together. And you create something beautiful together. But it's not anything that's planned. There are no rules for it. You make up the rules as you go along. And that's what doesn't work for me about this whole thing now with Emma. It's like there are rules for everything and all these expectations about what I'm supposed to do—about the part that I'm supposed to play. And there's just no room for me.

Dr. McKay: What are you supposed to do, Bill? What are all the rules and expectations that have suddenly become obvious? You've said that it wasn't this way before, when you were just visiting and spending the night together. When you were living in separate houses.

Bill: We took a lot of pleasure just in breaking any rules! We'd make love in the parking lot sometimes, outside the restaurant where Emma works. It was just fun. We were like two teenagers.

Dr. McKay: And so now, living together, it feels very different. What are the rules and expectations you have now that didn't exist a few months ago?

Bill: I'm supposed to come home at a certain time. Or, if I'm not coming home, I'm supposed to call her. I've got to have my guitars all in one place and not leave them around the house. I can't have friends over after a certain time, because it might keep her up, and they can't smoke in the house. She likes watching certain TV programs and likes me to be there to watch them with her. She doesn't like to do the grocery shopping by herself. I could go on and on.

Dr. McKay: So suddenly you're in a whole new world, and you're expected to live with boundaries and rules and a sense of structure you never had before in your relationship.

Bill: It's like instead of being in a jazz band, all of a sudden I'm in a symphony orchestra or something. And she's the conductor.

Dr. McKay: When you feel that she's the conductor and there are all these expectations you're suddenly expected to fulfill, what does it make you want to do?

Bill: It makes me want to leave—you know, go off and spend time by myself. Hang out with my musician friends.

Dr. McKay: You want to pull back and reestablish your independence in some way?

Bill: Yeah! And when it comes time to going to sleep, I just want to go to sleep.

Dr. McKay: And what do you feel if you can't do that—if you can't get away by yourself? You live in this house now with Emma. This is a life you share, and there's nowhere else to really go. And if you can't go anywhere else, you can't leave, and you can't get that sense that you're a little bit on your own, a little bit independent, what's the feeling that comes up?

Bill: Hopelessness and anger.

Dr. McKay: What effect do these feelings have on you?

Bill: It just feels like I'm getting smaller and smaller. I'm shrinking.

Dr. McKay: So you're shrinking, getting smaller and smaller. It's a very scary feeling. It's kind of depressing, too. And all you want to do is shut down and pull back into yourself and pull away from Emma. Because it feels like if you go toward Emma to connect, or to connect sexually, it's making it worse on some level.

Bill: It's like she has that much more power over me when we're connected like that. She's doing the conducting. I've got my eyes on her, and she's telling me what to play. I don't want to be in that role.

Dr. McKay: Okay. I can see how much pain there is for you in feeling like Emma's expectations are in effect controlling your life, orchestrating your life.

Bill: I'm just sick of it.

After several weeks of therapy, Bill was finally able to articulate the fear of engulfment lurking beneath his reluctance to engage sexually with Emma. It was then time to change the focus in our therapy dialogue to Emma's experience. Emma reported a lot of pain as she watched Bill withdraw. Her pain had a very particular quality—a sense of aloneness, a sense of hunger and of yearning.

Dr. McKay: Emma, when you are aware that Bill is pulling back physically, sexually, what happens inside you?

Emma: I begin to panic—a sense that I need him to connect with me. Because if he doesn't, it's like being completely unanchored. Like being in this cold space, without any light, without any walls. Like being in outer space.

Dr. McKay: You feel like you're in outer space. There's nothing around you, just a void. Emptiness.

Emma: I want a lifeline. And I thought that's what Bill was. I thought that's what our relationship was, a kind of lifeline to reel me back in. To make me feel my feet on the ground again.

Dr. McKay: And when he turns his back to you and stays on his side of the bed, when you can sense his withdrawal into himself, his resistance to opening to you—

Emma: I feel left out in the cold. And it makes me feel anxious and . . . sad.

Dr. McKay: And you're anxious because . . . What's going to happen? Let's imagine a future one or two or three years from now. You and Bill are still living together, and you are still living with this sense that Bill's turning away from you. I don't think that's going to be true, and we're here to change that. But let's for just a moment imagine that some time elapses, and you're still living with this kind of distance.

Emma: It's the worst kind of pain. I see myself getting older and feeling the sense of nothingness inside me, just wanting to fill it up—fill it up with someone, with something that has some meaning—so I won't have to feel that pain any more.

Dr. McKay: And can you stop the pain? Can you fill up that empty place inside you?

Emma: He used to be there for me, and there used to be ways we'd really connect. And now we don't, because he's shut that door. He's shut me out. And I just feel like we're in these two separate places even though we're living in the same house. We're completely separate.

Dr. McKay: And so you're completely separate, or it feels like you are. You can't connect in that deep way you used to, and you're in this relationship, in this life with Bill—

Emma: I'm stuck!

Dr. McKay: You're stuck?

Emma: I'm just stuck! It's only going to get worse. I mean, what's going to happen? I just feel this sense of wanting. It's like being hungry, but nothing you eat can touch that hunger.

Dr. McKay: So you're aiming for something, but you really can't have what you yearn for. You can't really turn to another person or another relationship, because you're in this relationship with Bill. But there's no way to get the nourishment you need. You see a life ahead of you with no way out. A life where you're going to be going hungry all the time. Is that right?

Emma: Yeah.

Bill and Emma were able to uncover, with a little prodding, the two core fears undermining their relationship: Bill's fear of engulfment and Emma's fear of emptiness. These intersecting fears were activated by their decision to live together. For Bill, living together set off a strong unconscious panic that his life would be sucked out of him, that he would be so regulated by Emma's requirements of him that all the things that matter to him—his tastes, his pleasures, his sustaining relationship to his music—would all come under Emma's control.

Bill's response was to shut down and withdraw into himself, to hoard whatever vestiges of independence he could find. And that shutting down, as so often occurs with couples who first move in together, affected the sexuality that had once been a source of closeness and pleasure between them.

Sexuality is the place where we can most easily merge and feel close; it is the place of our greatest power, but it is also the place of our greatest vulnerability in a relationship. The experience of merging sexually can feel like the foundation underpinning long-term love. But it can also feel extremely threatening, as it had come to feel to Bill, when the merging triggers an underlying fear of engulfment.

Not only does Bill feel like Emma wants to control him in his comings and goings and lifestyle, but his sense of her need to be close to him sexually activates his fear of engulfment even more, despite the fact that the sexual part of their relationship was once such a source of pleasure and satisfaction to him. As so often happens, Bill is using the bedroom as the battleground for what feels to him like a last desperate attempt to regain his independence.

Dr. McKay: Let me ask you this, Emma. In terms of intimacy and sexuality, is there anything you would like to change? If you had a magic wand and could change some things, what would you like to have different?

Emma: I'd like it to be the way it was when we were first seeing each other, before we lived together, when the relationship was really close and warm and loving and exciting.

Dr. McKay: That's the ideal. And that sounds wonderful. But now, given what you've heard from Bill and the kinds of struggles and fears and feelings he has, what would be realistic to hope for?

Emma: I guess I would hope that maybe he could focus more on me sometimes, on my needs and my desires. Just out of love for me.

Dr. McKay: He would focus on you. And how would he do that?

Emma: He'd pay attention to me. He'd put the guitar down, and he would see me. He'd listen to me maybe, for a change. And I could feel that sense that we were connected.

Dr. McKay: And how else could Bill very specifically nurture you, so that you felt more connected?

Emma: It's not like we have to have sex all the time. But I'd like him to hold me sometimes. You know, I'm on my feet all the time. It would be great if he gave me a foot rub sometimes or a back rub. It would mean a lot to me!

Dr. McKay: Sort of attend to you a little bit and pay attention to some of your physical needs—not just sexual needs but things that would just feel good.

Emma: Yeah.

Dr. McKay: Let me turn to you for a second, Bill. If we could wave a magic wand and the relationship could change a little bit, if things could change in a direction that would feel better for you, given all that you've heard from Emma and your awareness now of what some of her concerns are, how would you like the relationship to change?

Bill: I don't know. I want to have some room. I want to be able to just wait at the club until they call me up and I can sit in and not have to worry that I'm staying out too long, that she's going to be upset. I want to be home sometimes and just play with the guitar and work on something without feeling like she's waiting to talk to me, like she's just dying on the vine because I'm not paying attention to her. And when I get into bed, I just sink inside. Because I can feel how much she wants something. I need her to give me the room to come to *her*, instead of it being the other way around. To just give me the space to decide when I'm ready to connect, to feel close, to be touched.

This is an important juncture in our therapy dialogue. Both Bill and Emma are beginning to articulate some important needs in their relationship. And, as it turns out, these are very different needs, because Bill and Emma have very different fears.

A lot of the work of couple's therapy rests on the principle of equally valid needs. Two people who are struggling around a conflict—who appear to need very different things and, as in Bill and Emma's case, have very different fears underlying those needs— must be made to see that their respective needs, though different, are equally important, meaningful, valid, and legitimate. What happens so often in dysfunctional relationships is that one or both partners attempt to invalidate the other person's needs—to prove their partner's need to be insignificant or unimportant, to denigrate their partner's longing or fear.

The work of the therapy dialogue is to elevate each person's needs to a status of significance and importance. The couple must then as partners begin to look for ways to satisfy the different but equally valid needs that have thrown them into conflict.

Dr. McKay: We've reached an especially important point in our work, and I want to review where we've come so far. We were able to recognize that Bill, ever since the two of you moved in together, has been struggling because he feels his autonomy is threatened. He fears his ability to play music, to make his own schedule, pursue some of his own interests and pleasures is somehow in jeopardy—that Emma will attempt to control or orchestrate those needs. And, Bill, your response to that is to pull back into yourself, withdraw, and try to control the things you're able to control.

Emma, your fear is that you're going to be in that empty, lonely place where there's no closeness, no touch, no one who's looking at you, no one who cares. You're just out there by yourself, unanchored. And when Bill withdraws and there's less connection physically, sexually, all those fears are activated. And so your need is to find a way to get that closeness back, so that you're not alone anymore.

Bill, again, your need is to be able to have a sense of the integrity of your self—the sense that you have the right to exercise some choices and control in terms of your interests and desires, your schedule, when you make love and when you don't make love, all of that.

Now, given what we're learning about the underlying fears and the needs connected to them that are influencing this relationship and influencing what's going on sexually between you, I'm wondering if we can begin to think together about some solutions, some ways for the two of you to change how things work between you, so that we can to some degree reduce the fear and vulnerability that each of you feels and address some of the needs that each of you has told me about.

Emma: Is there any way that we could each have our nights? Maybe Mondays, Wednesdays, and Fridays we could spend together, and then—

Bill: I don't want to be on a schedule! That's just more control.

Emma: Well, how am I going to get my needs met at all if there isn't ever a time when you're going to pay attention to them? What do you suggest?

Bill: I don't know. But I don't want to be on a schedule. I don't want to be on the clock. I don't want to be required to make love to you just because it's Monday night.

Emma: Well, what makes you want to make love?

Bill: Feeling like I want to.

Emma: So I'm just left hanging and waiting.

Dr. McKay: Let me step in for a moment here. You're both express-ing some of the things that are very important parts of your needs and your fears. Emma, you don't want to be just waiting out there in empty space, feeling unanchored. And Bill, you don't want to feel controlled and made to live within a schedule or calendar. Both of those are very important needs. They're both completely valid and critical for us to acknowledge. Any solution we develop has to some-how take account of those needs, giving them equal weight.

Emma: If you can think of one, then you win the lottery. Because, as far as I can see, our equally valid needs just seem to cancel each other out.

Dr. McKay: Let's think about this. Emma, how could you give Bill some more room in this relationship to feel a little bit more like he had control over his schedule?

Emma: If he could give me more of what I need, I could give him more of what he needs. I wouldn't be demanding all the time if once in a while I got what I wanted.

Dr. McKay: So make a proposal. How could he give you a little more of what you need?

Emma: Well, he doesn't want to be on a timetable . . .

Dr. McKay: That was a perfectly reasonable idea, Emma, but it didn't quite fit for Bill. But let's continue to think. A lot of times the first thing we come up with is not the answer—it's not the idea that's going to work. That doesn't mean we can't find an answer.

Emma: What if I agree to lay off on asking him to check in with me and stuff like that? I have my classes, and I have plenty to do. I don't need to be with him every evening. I don't even want to be.

Dr. McKay: So no check-in? What does that mean?

Emma: He was complaining that he always has to let me know where he is and where he's been. And I don't really care about that so much. I've got my own stuff I'm doing.

Dr. McKay: So you'd be willing to relax a little bit the expectation that he check in regularly?

Emma: I think he thinks that I have more expectations about that than I really do. I don't care—so long as he's not doing something that would really be going against our relationship and our commitment to each other.

Dr. McKay: Do you support him going out and waiting to sit in at a club?

Emma: Yeah, sure. His life is his life.

Dr. McKay: And what do you need then? What would you hope for from him?

Emma: I'd hope that when he does spend time with me, I could feel that he was really loving me.

Dr. McKay: How could Bill express his love for you in a way that didn't make him feel *expected* to be turned on or sexual?

Emma: Like I said before, we could just cuddle or he could just look at me in a way that makes me feel appreciated.

Dr. McKay: He could cuddle with you or pay attention to you. How would he pay attention to you? Would he ask you questions or make eye contact?

Emma: I don't know. We could just have a meal together or something, or be in a situation where we were sitting across from each other. Maybe we could go out and have a meal, where someone else was serving the meal for a change!

Dr. McKay: So to be able to eat together and have conversations, to be in a situation in which you would feel he was paying attention to what was going on with you.

Emma: Yeah—share some time together.

Dr. McKay: Bill, what happens when you hear Emma's suggestion?

Bill: It sounds okay, I guess. I know she wants me to get in by a certain time at night. And, actually, I guess that's not even the issue, really. The issue is just feeling the whole time I'm away or the whole time even that I'm home playing the guitar or watching some stupid movie or whatever it is that doesn't involve her, that I'm doing the wrong thing. So if she's saying to me it's really okay to be in a club, waiting for a chance to sit in, hanging with some other musicians; if it's okay for me to play the guitar a little bit when I'm at home, and she's not going to freak out about that—I mean, that's really important to me! If I knew that was really true, I think I would feel different, somehow.

Emma: Well, it's really true. It's really true. You could do that.

Bill: I don't have a problem with having dinner together, really listening, trying to talk and have a conversation about what's going on with her, what's going on with me.

Emma: We could even go to one of your clubs where they play music you like.

Bill: I guess—I don't know. And, cuddling—what does that mean? The thing I'm afraid of is that if I'm really not into it, if I'm not in the mood, I don't want to be expected to go down to the finish line.

Emma: How about if we just agree that cuddling can just be cuddling sometimes—that it doesn't have to lead to anything else?

Dr. McKay: How could you signal Bill that you wanted to cuddle and you weren't expecting anything more—that you just wanted to be held and paid attention to and given some physical support, sweetness? How do you let him know that, so he doesn't have to worry that if he's not ready to be sexual on a given night, he can still cuddle with you and nothing more is expected of him?

Emma: When I was a kid, my mom used to say to us, "Hey, let's cuddle!" And we'd sit on the couch together and it was really nice. It was just a really close time.

Dr. McKay: And so you'd say to Bill, "Let's cuddle!" Bill, what if Emma said that to you and that was the signal that she just wanted to be close—not expecting more than that, but just to be physically close in a nonsexual way? How would that feel to you?

Bill: I think that's okay. I can do that. If I know that she's not going to be upset—like I'm disappointing her. If I know that's not where it's going to go, I'd be happy to cuddle with Emma. I care for Emma. I love Emma! If she wants to be held, I'd like to hold her.

Emma: That's really sweet, honey.

Therapist's Overview

Like a parakeet in a coal mine, sex is often the first thing to be affected when something goes wrong in a relationship. Commitment struggles and their related fears disrupt the delicate balance of intimacy and trust that supports good sex.

Bill and Emma are an example of how interlocking fears—in this case, those of engulfment and emptiness—can gang up on partners, each triggering the other. Bill's fear of engulfment gets activated when Emma complains about how preoccupied and unavailable he is and pressures him to be more intimate. Emma's fear of emptiness gets set off by Bill's needs for independence, which leave her feeling disconnected and alone. The more Emma asks for, the less Bill wants to give—and sex becomes the arena of conflict.

What to do? It won't help to keep struggling about sex. That's just the top layer of the problem. Like Emma and Bill, you have to begin with an assessment of your underlying fears and needs. Try interviewing each other about your sexual conflicts, using the Couples Research Form.

Couples Research Form

Issue/Conflict: _____

_____

Fears: *What does my partner fear might happen?* _____

_____

Other feelings my partner has about this issue: _____

_____

History: *What are my partner's experiences from the past (this or other relationships or childhood experiences) that relate to this issue?* _____

_____

Assumptions: *What are my partner's beliefs about this issue— about what will happen in the future; about my motives, feelings, and intentions?* _____

_____

Perceived choices: *What options does my partner believe he or she has regarding this issue?* _____

_____

Needs: *What does my partner want and need?* _____

_____

Adapted from *When Anger Hurts Your Relationship* by Kim Paleg, Ph.D., and Matthew McKay, Ph.D. Used by permission.

Action Plan #1: Fill Out the Couples Research Form

You can do this exercise alone or with your partner.

First write a brief, neutral description of the problem as you each see it. If you're working with your partner, pass the description back and forth between you until you come up with something that seems accurate to both of you. "We have different ideas about how often we want to have sex" is an example of a description that's simple and nonjudgmental.

Now ask your partner questions about each item on the form. If you're working alone, go through the form twice—once for yourself and once role-playing your partner with as much empathy and accuracy as you can muster.

Under *fears*, you might ask:

- What are you afraid will happen if our conflict over sex continues?
- What are you afraid would happen if I got my way?
- What's your biggest nightmare about what's going to happen (to you, to me, to us) when this issue comes up?

Under *other feelings*, you could ask:

- Do you have other feelings that come up in connection to the issue of sex?
- Do you feel hurt, sad, guilty, overwhelmed, ashamed, and/or betrayed about this?
- What's the most difficult feeling that comes up for you around this issue?

Under *history*, there are a couple of key questions you can ask:

- Has anything ever happened to you in the past—either between us or with someone else—that is affecting you with regard to the issue of sex?
- Have you ever been through anything before that feels like this?

Under *assumptions*, you can ask several or all of the following questions:

- How do you see our conflict over sex? What's your point of view?
- What's your view of my behavior in regard to this issue?

- What do you think is going to happen to us in the future as we continue to confront this issue?
- What's your sense of my motives and/or feelings?

Under *perceived choices*, try asking these questions:

- What options or choices do you think we have in this situation?
- Is there a choice you might make that you think I'd find unacceptable?

Under *needs*, ask your partner:

- What do you need in order to make this situation less of a conflict for you?
- What's the most important thing you need changed?
- What's one thing that would make you feel better?
- If things were exactly the way you wanted them, how would they be?

When you ask these questions, use a separate piece of paper to write down the main things your partner says in response. Don't correct, refute, or criticize anything he or she tells you. Pretend you're a journalist, someone getting facts for a story. (This means you *can* ask for clarification.) Your job is to listen and understand, not to editorialize about what you've heard.

As soon as one interview is complete, reverse the process. The interviewer becomes the interviewee and answers all the questions he or she just asked.

Here's an example of how two of my clients, a couple in their thirties who had two young children, used the Couples Interview Form:

Yoshiko: What are you afraid will happen if this situation continues?

Ken: I'm afraid we'll drift apart and eventually get a divorce.

Yoshiko: What are you afraid would happen if I got my way on this issue?

Ken: We'll lose the closeness and intimacy of our marriage. We'll become more like siblings than husband and wife.

Yoshiko: What's your biggest nightmare about what's going to happen (to you, to me, to us) when this issue comes up?

Ken: Being stuck in a loveless marriage. Having to go against my values, to cheat on you or to leave you. Not being able to be with our children any more, being shut out of their lives.

Yoshiko: Do you feel hurt, sad, guilty, overwhelmed, ashamed, and/or betrayed about this?

Ken: I feel all of those feelings.

Yoshiko: Has anything ever happened to you in the past, either between us or with someone else, that is affecting you with regard to this issue?

Ken: I keep thinking about how things were before the kids were born. We were happy being lovers—at least, I always thought you seemed happy with me. And now I'm wondering whether even that was real.

Yoshiko: What's your view of my behavior in regard to this issue?

Ken: I keep thinking that maybe you're just tired. Maybe you're overwhelmed.

Yoshiko: What's your sense of my motives and/or feelings?

Ken: The kids take a lot of your energy. Maybe you just want to keep your body for yourself during the times when they're not making demands of you.

Yoshiko: What options or choices do you think we have in this situation?

Ken: Because we want to stay together, I guess I just have to wait. Or maybe we can work out some kind of compromise until the kids are a little older.

Yoshiko: Is there a choice you might make that you think I'd find unacceptable?

Ken: Cheating, I guess. I don't like the idea either.

Yoshiko: What do you need to make this situation less of a conflict for you?

Ken: I need closeness and intimacy with you. I need to feel like you're my wife again, that you're my lover again.

Yoshiko: What's one thing that would make you feel better?

Ken: Maybe you could just feel more open to being naked together and hugging. I miss you—I miss your body. I'd like it if you didn't wear so many clothes to bed.

Yoshiko: If things were exactly the way you wanted them, how would they be?

Ken: We'd be great parents, and great lovers, too. We wouldn't forget that it was our love for each other that brought our children into the world.

The Couples Research Form can yield a huge amount of information, giving you new insights about your partner's and perhaps your own feelings and needs (even if you've worked by yourself in doing the exercise). Building respect for each other's wants and emotions will help you face your sexual conflicts with empathy rather than blame.

Action Plan #2: Role Reversal

Now that you know a lot more about each other's fears and needs, it's time to start working on solutions. Instead of advocating for your own position, we suggest you reverse roles.

This exercise can work whether or not your partner is participating. If you're playing both roles, set up two chairs facing each other.

If participating alone, sit in one chair when you're advocating your own position, and the other chair when you're advocating your partner's position.

Using what you've learned about your partner from the Couples Research Form, try to represent his or her position. Suggest solutions to the conflict that truly reflect what your partner feels and needs.

If you're working with your partner, set an egg timer for ten minutes. While it's ticking, talk about the issue together, remaining in your switched roles. Be good advocates. Explain why you (playing the role of your partner) feel the way you do. Explain how your (your partner's) past experience affects your reactions and needs.

After each of you has had a chance to talk, reset the timer for an additional ten minutes. Stay with the role reversal, but this time each of you should offer a compromise solution that takes into account both of your needs.

A solution in which one person wins and the other loses won't work; a solution that satisfies only one partner's needs is also bound to fail. Keep talking about your problem-solving ideas until one of them—or maybe some combination of them—feels good to both of you.

Don't expect this process to be easy or painless. It will require a high degree of empathy and goodwill from each of you. If the situation becomes too painful or too charged, take a break, resolving to return to the exercise at a later time when you're both feeling relaxed and calm.

9

Exclusivity

Who Do We Let In, Who Do We Keep Out?

The message on my machine was spoken in a clear female voice with a strong Southern accent. "Other people are getting in the way of our marriage. We need your help, if it's not already too late."

Seth and Georgia were both in their fifties when they came to see me. They'd been married three years. This was a second marriage for Seth and the first for Georgia.

Georgia described herself as an executive assistant. She was well spoken and took obvious care with her appearance; I could imagine her being a source of pride to the person she worked for. She carried with her a bit of an air of superiority, which I noticed as she brushed some invisible specks of dust or crumbs off my leather chair before she smiled at me and sat down.

Seth worked as a tool wholesaler for a large national firm. He had the sheepish look men sometimes get in middle age, as if he expected people to criticize him and hoped he could join them in a laugh instead, even if it was at his own expense. He seemed like a kind-hearted person, an innocent, someone who just wanted to have a good time and get by with the least effort possible.

Georgia's contempt of Seth was palpable; she'd gotten to the point where she could barely stand to be around him, she was that fed up. I could see that Seth was hoping they could just get this therapy over with as soon as possible, with the least possible pain.

Sometimes, when people come in, I just want to run and hide because it seems right off the bat like I'm not going to be able to do anything to help them, no matter how much I want to. I took a deep breath and invited Seth and Georgia to make themselves comfortable.

Seth and Georgia's Commitment Dialogue

Dr. McKay: Let's start by talking about what brings you in today.

Georgia: I have one word: Sammy!

Seth: Well, I have two words: Mary Lee!

Dr. McKay: Let me understand what you're both telling me. There are two people in your lives, Sammy and Mary Lee, who are a problem in your relationship?

Georgia: Yup. Sammy, Seth's best friend since he was fourteen years old. Sammy's always at our house. Seth's always hanging out with him, going out with him, going on vacation. I mean, you'd think those two were married.

Seth: Wait a minute! Those aren't vacations. We just go out twice a year and see a baseball game at different parks around the country. It's something we've been doing for years.

Georgia: I wish there was something like that *we* could point to that we've been doing together for years. Is there anything like that?

Dr. McKay: I'm going to ask you to hold on while I interrupt for a second. Again, what I'm hearing is that there are two people in your lives who are having an impact on the quality of your relationship. Let me start with you, Georgia. Tell me a little bit about what you're experiencing with Seth and Sammy. And, Seth, I want to hear about your experience with Mary Lee in a minute.

Georgia: When I first started seeing Seth, he was really wonderful. I have a lot of respect and admiration for him, a lot of love for him.

But when he's around Sammy, and that's about 50 percent of the time, he turns into a different person!

Dr. McKay: It's Jekyll and Hyde?

Georgia: Yeah! Here we have a fifty-five-year-old man who transforms into an obnoxious fifteen-year-old boy. And I feel like their mom or something.

Dr. McKay: What happens when Seth is with Sammy that you don't like?

Georgia: Where should I begin? There are the card games, for one. You wouldn't believe the level of juvenile behavior. Who can burp the loudest. Who can—I won't even say what they do! This man Sammy has a laugh that shreds my nerves. When he walks into the house, I walk straight to the medicine cabinet and take two aspirin.

Dr. McKay: So there's a quality of the laughter and card games—

Georgia: It's also what he brings out in Seth. It's like this part of him I never see except when Sammy's around. And it's a part of him I never want to see! I don't even recognize him. It's the constant sports; the beer drinking; the mindless, violent movies. Then they're off to play pinball. I mean, these are two grown men acting like kids. And I like kids just fine, but not when they're bald on top and have love handles.

Dr. McKay: I see. Seth, you mentioned someone named Mary Lee. What's her part in your relationship with Georgia?

Seth: Mary Lee! That's Georgia's sister. She's always coming over, supposedly to watch TV with Georgia. But it turns into a big bitch session about what's wrong with me—I can hear them in there. It's one criticism after another. Mary Lee has always had it out for me. She can hardly even bring herself to be polite, and I know she's poisoned the well of our marriage.

Dr. McKay: Seth, let me ask you this. When Georgia and Mary Lee are sitting in front of the TV and talking about your relationship, what happens inside of you? What's your emotional reaction as you hear their voices in the other room?

Seth: Well, I feel small. I feel like there's nothing right about me.

Dr. McKay: What's the emotion that fits that experience?

Seth: I don't know what you'd call the emotion. But it's just not right for somebody to come in and turn your own wife against you. I know they're sisters and all, but there's something really messed up about that.

Dr. McKay: I understand what you're saying, that there's something about this that really disturbs you. I'm wondering what that feeling is like when you hear them talking in the next room and you know they're talking about you. What's happening inside of you?

It took several sessions before Seth could put a name to the uncomfortable feelings he was experiencing.

I've noticed in my work that a lot of men have been so put down by their parents and society at large for having painful, embarrassing, or even overly exuberant feelings — "Don't be silly, there's nothing to be afraid of!" "What a crybaby!" "Control yourself!" — that they've learned the habit of disowning or invalidating those feelings. Whereas many girls in our society grow up conversant in the language of feelings, a lot of men have to struggle immensely to connect words to the emotional experiences they've so successfully tamped down or buried. Such lifelong adaptations are difficult to overcome.

Here is a continuation of Seth and Georgia's therapy dialogue, two sessions later.

Seth: I don't know what the feeling is exactly. I feel like they're making fun of me or something.

Dr. McKay: They're making fun of you. And the emotion that goes with that, with feeling like you're the object of their humor, of some kind of judgment they're making—what is that feeling?

Seth: It's a bad feeling. It's a feeling like I'm messed up. I'm stupid. I'm some dumb hick from Texas who talks wrong, likes the wrong things, has got no taste, and has the wrong friends. Like the whole thing between me and Georgia was just one big mistake.

Dr. McKay: When you're listening to the two of them talk, you feel kind of ashamed—like you're not okay, and your friends aren't okay. Like there's something wrong with you?

Seth: Yeah, I guess that's about it.

Dr. McKay: Let me ask you something else. What would it be like for you if Sammy wasn't in your life? If somehow, tomorrow, he disappeared from your life and just wasn't there anymore—what would life feel like then?

Seth: It just wouldn't be the same. It'd feel dark. Sammy is like a bright light. He makes me laugh, he makes me feel happy to be alive. It's always been like that, since we were kids. It would just feel dark in the world without him, like the sunshine was gone.

Georgia: Wow! I think you're living with the wrong person, Seth. If the doctor asked you about how you'd feel if I disappeared from the world, I doubt you'd have anything near so sentimental to say about me.

Seth: I love you! I love you, Georgia. But it *is* different. You know the story, babe—Sammy and I have been best friends since we were kids. We've always had a great time when we're together—always have, always will. That doesn't mean I don't love you . . .

Georgia: I don't know what it does mean, when you say you love me. It doesn't seem to mean anything!

Dr. McKay: Georgia, what you're saying is very important. You're saying, if I understand you correctly, that Sammy—and Sammy's presence in your life—is telling you something about your value and worth and who you are to Seth. I want to get back to that. But I want to see if we can finish up and understand a little bit more about what would happen for Seth if Sammy were not in his life. Because that's something I also want to understand. So, Seth, if Sammy weren't around, if tomorrow he were to disappear, are you saying that life would feel emptier? Like there was some source of light and laughter that wouldn't be there anymore?

Seth: Yeah. It just wouldn't be the same without him.

Dr. McKay: Okay. So, on the one hand, Sammy and Sammy's presence in your life gives you this feeling of joy, of this long-standing connection that you enjoy deeply and have grown to count on and that makes you really happy. And anything that would threaten that would make you feel like the source of that was going to get lost, and you were going to be in an emptier, darker life.

Seth: Yeah.

Dr. McKay: Georgia, let me get back to you now. You started to talk about what Sammy's presence in your life means to you, and what it means in terms of your relationship to Seth. Tell me more about that.

Georgia: When I hear Seth talking now about his feelings for Sammy and what a light Sammy is for his world and what joy he brings him, I don't even know why I'm sitting here. I don't even know why we're here! I feel like I don't even matter to Seth. I feel like I'm like the piece of parsley you get on your plate—something that's not really part of the meal. It sounds like what really matters to Seth is something that happened a long time ago in his relationship with Sammy—not with me! How can I compete? I came into Seth's life three years ago. How can I compete with somebody who goes back to the time when he was fourteen? It's like Sammy's the lifeline to Seth's boyhood memories. I don't have any sort of function like that in Seth's life.

Dr. McKay: What are you afraid might happen with you and Seth?

Georgia: I think that I could step off the face of the earth, and it really wouldn't make that much difference to Seth. And I feel like he might disappear at any time. I think he likes me just fine, but I don't think he has that sense of connection with me that he has with Sammy. I just don't think there's anything like that between us.

Dr. McKay: You're afraid you might lose him.

Georgia: Yeah. I feel like I don't even *have* him to lose.

Dr. McKay: So what Sammy means to you is that Seth already has a very strong relationship that gives him the support and the happiness that he needs. And his relationship with you is just a little extra that he can easily let go of.

Seth: I don't know where this is coming from, Georgia! You know I treat you well. You know I think about you. I do things with you. We spend time talking and hanging out.

Georgia: Not much!

Seth: I look after your car. And I'm always trying to think of things that could make you happy. I bought you that bread maker you wanted. I'm always doing stuff for you. I don't understand this!

Georgia: I don't see you talking about me as the light in your life! You talk about Sammy, and your eyes get bright, but they don't get bright when you talk about me. Yeah, we hang out, and we spend time together. But I always feel like it's kind of a drag for you, and you're putting in time. Like you're punching the clock.

Seth: That's not true! I like being with you when you and Mary Lee are not hanging around talking about how screwed up I am!

Georgia: I invite Mary Lee over, or she tends to come by, when you and Sammy are doing your thing together.

Dr. McKay: Let me just interrupt you both for a minute. I know these are deeply felt issues. But I want to understand better what's happening with both of you. Georgia, I want to stay focused on what it feels like with Sammy in your life. So one thing is the sense that you're not very important and Seth could leave at any time. The relationship could fall apart, and it wouldn't matter to him. You described yourself earlier in the session as "the parsley on the plate"—nothing really essential. Something he could lose but not miss terribly much. You feel dispensable.

Georgia: Easily. But Mary Lee is my big sister. She's always been there for me. She stands by me, she really does! I know she loves me. That's unconditional. I don't feel that Seth has that kind of love for me.

Dr. McKay: Let me ask you something else. When you look at Sammy and the kinds of things that Seth and Sammy do together—the sports, the violent movies, the pinball and the card games, and that laugh that Sammy has—what does that mean about *you*? That you're with Seth, and Seth and Sammy like to do these things?

Georgia: I feel embarrassed to be around them. I feel ashamed! Look at them—they're acting like a couple of teenagers with pimples. I mean, isn't it time that Seth grew up?

Dr. McKay: So it's embarrassing to see them acting so young together—

Georgia: So immature!

Dr. McKay: So that kind of laughing and carrying on feels very immature. What does it mean about you? You're with Seth, and Seth is having this kind of relationship with Sammy. Does that say anything about you that feels uncomfortable?

Georgia: Well, don't I deserve to be with a grown-up man?

Dr. McKay: And if you're not with a grown-up man, if you're with a man who likes to hang out with someone like Sammy and likes to do the things that Seth and Sammy do together—

Georgia: It makes me feel that all the work I've done in my life just goes to hell as soon as that man walks through our door.

Dr. McKay: You said you're embarrassed. It's as if who you are and what you've worked so hard to achieve in your life is all kind of washed away by the silliness in their relationship?

Georgia: It just brings me back to the worst parts of being a kid and being the little sister, the baby sister. The one who's immature, who doesn't know what's what. Who's not sophisticated.

Dr. McKay: So when they're being very silly and acting very young, on some level it makes you feel left out, not part of things, kind of marginalized in the way you may have felt when you were a child—

Georgia: It's weird, because it makes me feel left out, but it's not something I even want to be part of. But I do feel left out! What I feel left out of is that part of Seth I really love. It's like there's this special room that Sammy takes Seth into, this kind of make-believe room, which is the Sammy room and where they're just goofy together. And Seth leaves his grown-up self behind.

Dr. McKay: So you feel embarrassed. You feel left out. And you feel like you're in danger, like Seth could drift away and maybe not even miss you.

Georgia: I do. I guess I feel like he'll just stay in that Sammy room, and I'll be left out, on the outside.

Dr. McKay: And, Seth, when you're listening to Georgia, what's happening for you right now?

Seth: I don't even know what she's talking about. I mean, yes, Sammy and I have a good time. So what's the big deal? I just think it's that crap that Mary Lee puts into her head every night. If she's not over at our house watching television with Georgia, they're on the phone together.

Georgia: What you don't get is that Mary Lee is my support system, and she's there for me in ways that you have not been there.

Seth: I don't even understand that. I do lots of things with you. Yeah, Sammy comes over. But when you and I are together—we're talking, we're hanging out, we're having nice dinners together. You know, we're having a good time!

Georgia: But Mary Lee actually cares about what's good for me. She takes the trouble to understand what's important to me.

Dr. McKay: Let me just interrupt again. I think you're both in a lot of pain here. On the one hand, Seth, you're feeling like an object of ridicule. We talked about the feeling of shame that Mary Lee and Georgia are looking at you and looking at your relationship with Sammy and perhaps judging it—evaluating you as not grown up enough. And there's also this feeling that, without Sammy, life would be emptier. There would be less joy in your life, and that's something you don't want to have happen. And, Georgia, you're feeling like Seth is kind of caught in this arrested development, and it embarrasses you to see this teenage relationship between two fifty-five-year-old men. But worse, perhaps, is this feeling that you don't matter and Seth could easily leave you or let go of you, because he has most of what he needs with his old boyhood friend.

At this point we're starting to get a clearer picture of the fears underlying Seth and Georgia's conflict. Seth's relationship to Sammy is deep and long and very satisfying, presumably, to both men. It has the elements of their juvenile selves, years ago, growing up together. The experience of the relationship is one of light and exuberance and joy. The thought of shutting Sammy out of his life makes Seth feel a great sense of loss or emptiness. Georgia's attempts to limit their relationship are running up against Seth's love for Sammy and the emptiness he would feel if the relationship were curtailed.

Besides Seth's fear of emptiness, we're beginning to understand his feelings about Georgia and Mary Lee. He feels judged, ridiculed, embarrassed—a fear of shame is propelling Seth's angry attacks on Mary Lee and her relationship to Georgia.

On Georgia's end, she feels superfluous, unimportant, and vulnerable to abandonment. It feels like Seth and Sammy can go on very well without her. But there's something else. Seth and Sammy together seem like young boys, and their exuberance, their laughter, the cards, the violent movies, the pinball all seem to Georgia slightly lowbrow. She's embarrassed, even ashamed, to be around it. And she wants to push Sammy out of their lives—for the very same reason, in fact, that Seth would like to push Mary Lee out of their lives.

Sammy and Mary Lee are sources of emotional sustenance but also sources of shame for both Seth and Georgia.

Dr. McKay: You've told me some of the things you're struggling with, and I know that you came here not just to tell me what the problem is, but to make some changes so that the problem can be resolved. I want to tell you that the problem is not as much with the role Mary Lee and Sammy play in your lives as with the relationship between you two. I think we need to pay attention to what's going on in your relationship and how to make that relationship really thrive. And when it can thrive, then Sammy and Mary Lee are going to have a very diminished impact. Seth, from what you've said over the last few weeks, it sounds as if there's a lot of good in your relationship with Georgia. But for the part that doesn't work, the core experience is that of feeling judged and ashamed. Is that right?

Seth: Yeah, basically.

Dr. McKay: All right. Let me turn to you, Georgia. There are good things in this relationship for you, too. But there are also some very negative and painful parts that you've come here to work on. If you were going to choose one word to describe what's not working in this relationship and the negative experience you're feeling with it, what would that one word be?

Georgia: It's the same way I'm feeling right now in this therapy session—unimportant!

Dr. McKay: So you feel unimportant in the relationship. But you also feel unimportant in the therapy session. Tell me more about that.

Georgia: I just feel like it's all about Seth and Sammy. It's not about me and Seth at all. I feel like I just don't matter.

Dr. McKay: Now I want to kind of leave Sammy out of this for a minute, if I can. And I think maybe you'd like to also. Leaving Sammy out, what would you need to have happen between you and Seth to feel like you're important to him?

Georgia: I'd like to see him light up when he's around me, like he lights up when he's around Sammy. I'd like to feel that if I dropped dead tomorrow, it would actually make some kind of difference to him.

Dr. McKay: What do you and Seth do together that gives you a chance to feel Seth's joy in your presence?

Georgia: Sometimes I feel like the only thing I can give him that Sammy can't give him is sex.

Dr. McKay: So that's one of the things. Do you see his joy then?

Georgia: Yup. He enjoys that.

Dr. McKay: So that's one of the times you feel his joy. Are there any other times when you feel his pleasure in the relationship between the two of you?

Georgia: Not really.

Dr. McKay: What do you do together? What kinds of activities do you share?

Georgia: We don't have that many common interests, to tell you the truth. We don't like the same TV programs. I'm always trying to get him to go to some of the cultural events I like going to, but he never wants to go. And I have no interest in going to the kinds of things he's interested in.

Dr. McKay: Okay. So part of what's happening here is that you do have very different interests! And so far you haven't had an opportunity to explore which interests, which experiences, you could share and get some enjoyment from together.

Georgia: Well, we both work. And when we have time at home together, we end up both watching TV but in different rooms. And that's often when I have my sister come over, and Seth is often hanging out with Sammy.

Dr. McKay: What would happen in the relationship, do you think, in terms of how it feels to you, if you and Seth shared more together, more interests that you actually pursued in common?

Georgia: I think it would be great. It might make me feel that I mattered to him a little or that I was a source of pleasure to him, too— beyond just sex.

Dr. McKay: You'd feel more important to Seth if there were more activities and experiences you could share.

Georgia: I'd not only feel more important to him, but he'd feel better to me, as a partner. It would feel more right. I've got to say, it's not really feeling very right to me.

Dr. McKay: And, Seth, this experience of being judged, evaluated, and not feeling good enough. What would need to change in your relationship for that feeling of being judged to diminish?

Seth: Well, maybe if Mary Lee was not around so much or they weren't talking on the phone so much! Or they weren't talking about me all the time.

Dr. McKay: Let's leave Mary Lee out of it for a minute. What would have to change in your relationship to Georgia for you to have the confidence that she values and respects you? What would have to change there?

Seth: I guess she'd have to say that to me. Or she'd have to stop all her complaining.

Dr. McKay: Seth, what do you long for in your relationship to Georgia?

Seth: I don't know . . . I wish she liked me! I just wish she liked who I am, not because of what I do but because of who I am.

Dr. McKay: How would she convey that to you? How could she help you know that she likes and values who you are?

Seth: She could just tell me she likes me. She could tell me the things she likes about me, instead of telling me what an idiot I am and asking me when Sammy's going to leave and all that crap. I never hear anything that she likes about me. It's only just what's wrong with me.

Dr. McKay: So you need to hear what Georgia sees in you—to mirror back to you the things she sees that she really loves, that she recognized when she first met you, that set you apart from other people, that made you the one for her. Is that right?

Seth: Yeah, I'd like to hear her be positive about me for a change. I want her to stop complaining about me all the time. Why does it have to be so heavy? Why can't we just have fun sometimes, and not focus on what's wrong with us and what's wrong with me and Sammy?

Dr. McKay: Listening to both of you, I have a very strong feeling that you're asking each other for exactly the same thing. You're asking for a chance to share a life with each other in which you both feel valued, approved of, and enjoyed. So I want to ask both of you right now, how are we going to do that? Georgia wants to feel important. She wants to feel that she shares more of your life, Seth. And you want to feel valued and know that she really sees what's good and special in you. How are we going to go about making that happen?

Seth: I don't know.

Georgia: I don't know either. I can't think of a way.

Dr. McKay: All right. Let me think out loud with you for a minute. Seth, you're not going to give up your relationship to Sammy. You're lifelong friends, going back forty years. And, Georgia, you're not going to stop being close to your sister. She means too much to you. The problem is that you're both focusing on these other people instead of focusing on the two of you. How are you going to build a relationship that works between you? Georgia, Seth needs to know that he's not an object of ridicule and judgment. And, Seth, Georgia needs to know that she's really important to you. You don't have to give up these other important people in your lives. But some changes have to be made to make your relationship together your highest priority. What can we do so, Seth, you can feel valued and special, and, Georgia, you can feel important and central in Seth's life? What might we do to make that happen?

Georgia: When we were first going out, when we first met, I was impressed with the way Seth really listened to me. He really took in what I said. He listened with interest. And if he showed even some part of that interest in me now, it would make a huge difference to me. It seems like so much of our focus these days is about him and about what he's doing, and so much of what he's doing I don't like. But it's like what I think about, what I want to do, doesn't even enter into the picture. I'd really like him to listen, to be more attentive to me again. More interested. To look at me like there's a little bit of undiscovered territory here.

Dr. McKay: And yet you have very few things that you do in common right now. That's part of what the problem has been for you, that Seth and Sammy have many things in common, that they share, but the two of you haven't developed many common interests.

Georgia: I feel like I can't compete with those forty years of friendship. We've known each other for just over three years. How can I compete?

Dr. McKay: Suppose the two of you made a commitment to really building that structure between you—things you enjoy, things that you share with each other? Seth, you need Sammy; and, Georgia, you need your sister. But they're taking up too much room in your relationship, and they're crowding out the time and the emotional closeness that you need to build—something permanent and strong and lasting—between you. Let me ask you this: You've been going through some hard times. Do you want to stay together? Do you want to work at that? Do you want to make this relationship between you the highest priority, the thing that you really care about and put first?

Georgia: I guess if I didn't, I wouldn't be sitting here now.

Dr. McKay: And what about you, Seth?

Seth: I love my wife. I wouldn't be here either if I didn't love my wife. I'm sick of her sister, but I want to be with Georgia.

Dr. McKay: Okay then. Let me go back to this question of how we're going to build this connection between the two of you that's satisfying and feels good. And we're going to need to start by developing new, shared experiences that you can both be committed to and both learn to enjoy with each other.

Over a period of ten weeks, we discovered more and more activities that Seth and Georgia could share. As they enjoyed more together, they felt closer, more connected. And as their intimacy increased, sister and best friend became less and less likely to trigger resentment for either of them.

Therapist's Overview

Sometimes it can feel like your relationship gets awfully crowded. Instead of just the two of you, there's a cast of unwanted characters pushing themselves into your life. Or, worse still, your partner seems to be welcoming someone else into your relationship, betraying the primacy of your bond.

The issue of exclusivity—who you will let in or keep out of your life as a couple—becomes a nexus for struggle between many partners. The problem often shows up as you first encounter a lover's key relationships. These people, family or friends, have provided a base of intimacy and support long before you arrived on the scene. They've done and shared so much with your partner that their influence may reach right into your bedroom. Some typical scenarios include:

- Friends or family who need your partner's help and suck a lot of time and energy.
- Good-time comrades who may have more in common with your partner than you do. They always seem to be off together having fun—sharing hobbies, sports, nights out— while you wait at home, feeling left out.
- Pseudo affairs—people for whom your partner has a lot of sexual and emotional juice. They're not sleeping together, but

it feels like they might as well be. You see their shared attraction and a level of emotional intimacy that makes them seem more like lovers than friends.

- Confidants with whom your partner shares intimate details of your relationship. It feels embarrassing and/or shameful to have someone know so much. These may be problems you'd like your partner to solve with you, not someone else. Moreover, the advice your partner gets may be exerting an unwanted influence on your life.

The issue of exclusivity doesn't just pertain to preexisting relationships. It can also be triggered by people who suddenly enter your lives. The flaring up of a new intimacy, a newly discovered friend who shares one of your partner's passions, or a friend from work who suddenly is spending a lot of time at your house can all set off alarm bells. And the more you try to limit these relationships, the more some partners will dig in their heels and insist on their innocence as well as their importance.

When your partner or spouse brings unwanted people into your life, it can trigger a strong fear response. Like Seth, you may struggle with a fear of shame as information about your flaws and failings is paraded before someone who seems poised to judge you. Or, like Georgia, you may fear abandonment as you watch your partner revel in a friendship whose charms are an utter mystery to you. The fear of emptiness can also come into play: you may feel increasingly lonely and cut off while your partner pours time and energy into others.

It can feel like an outrage when your partner shows a need for emotional closeness to someone other than you. Aren't you both supposed to be enough for each other? Why would a really committed partner spend so much of his or her precious personal time and energy outside the primary love relationship? Why do some partners push so hard and insistently to include unwanted people in their lives?

There are as many answers as there are individual situations. Most people feel a simple, healthy need to maintain a network of support and friendship that extends beyond that provided by their primary relationship. It's very difficult, if not impossible, for one person, no matter how loved, to be everything to his or her partner. Maintaining or creating closeness to other people can be a way to balance the forces pulling toward merger with a little healthy autonomy.

But when a partner seems to invest an excessive amount of time and energy in outside relationships to the detriment of his or her own life with you, there's usually one underlying emotion: the fear of engulfment.

People typically manage this fear by means of three main coping strategies: triangulation, distancing, and disappearing.

Triangulation occurs when a partner directs high levels of energy and interest toward a third person. Sometimes this is sexual, sometimes emotional. But either way, the result is a reduction in closeness between the original partners.

Distancing strategies include coldness, withdrawal, and picking fights. Bringing unwanted people into your relationship is a perfect opportunity for distancing, because it will very predictably trigger conflict. The more you complain about the objectionable person, the more you relieve your partner's fears about engulfment. The fighting provides exactly what he or she was looking for—emotional space.

Disappearing is an oft-used strategy to cope with engulfment. (We say "strategy" but, of course, none of these are conscious strategies. They're just paths we instinctively take to bring us relief from our emotional pain.) A good way to disappear is to hang out with third parties. The more time people who fear engulfment spend away from their partners, the less engulfment feels like an issue to them.

So what does this all mean for your relationship? If there's triangulation, distancing, or disappearing via relationships to third parties, you can assume that an underlying fear motivates the behavior. To begin overcoming the struggle around exclusivity, we suggest you look beyond the specifics of the conflict to the fears and needs that motivate each of you. Start by filling out the Couples Research Form that follows.

Couples Research Form

Issue/Conflict: _____

_____

Fears: *What does my partner fear might happen?* _____

_____

Other feelings my partner has about this issue: _____

_____

History: *What are my partner's experiences from the past (this or other relationships or childhood experiences) that relate to this issue?* _____

_____

Assumptions: *What are my partner's beliefs about this issue—about what will happen in the future; about my motives, feelings, and intentions?* _____

_____

Perceived choices: *What options does my partner believe he or she has regarding this issue?* _____

_____

Needs: *What does my partner want and need?* _____

_____

Adapted from *When Anger Hurts Your Relationship* by Kim Paleg, Ph.D., and Matthew McKay, Ph.D. Used by permission.

Action Plan #1: Fill Out the Couples Research Form

You can do this exercise by yourself, role-playing your partner's point of view, even if he or she isn't willing to participate. The exercise will still yield useful information.

If you're working with your partner, begin the process by creating a brief neutral description of your problem regarding exclusivity in your relationship. There's a good chance you'll have difficulty with this, because you may see the problem very differently. Here are some ideas to help you write a description that will feel fair and accurate to both of you.

One of you should begin by writing a brief description of the problem (just a phrase or two) on a separate piece of paper. "Our disagreement about the role [name of person] plays in our lives . . ." is a good example of wording that's direct and noncombative. It is important to use language that carries no judgment or blame.

Now let your partner read your description and rewrite it, if necessary, to accurately reflect his or her view of the problem as well. Make sure this revised description remains neutral and accurate. Continue the process, passing the draft back and forth, until you have a description that seems fair to both of you.

Now start the actual interview. You can flip a coin to see who gets interviewed first; but it doesn't matter, because you'll both get a turn to express your point of view.

Starting with *fears*, ask your partner:

- What are you afraid would be the effect on our relationship, our future, and your well-being if [my/your] relationship to [name of person] continues to play such a large role in our life?

Moving on to *other feelings*, ask your partner:

- Do you have other feelings that come up around this issue?
- What's your strongest feeling (such as jealousy, fear, frustration, or anger) regarding this issue? Can you go into more detail?

In terms of *history*, ask one or more of these questions:

- What experiences from your past have influenced your attitudes about who we include in our lives?
- While you were growing up, did you and/or your parents have conflicts about people brought into the family circle?
- Is there an event we've experienced together that influences your attitude and feelings about [name of person]?

Under *assumptions*, ask your partner some or all of the following questions:

- In a nutshell, how would you characterize our conflict about [name of person]? What do you think is the main cause of the problem?
- What's your sense of what makes me feel the way I do about [name of person]?
- How do you think our issues about [name of person] will affect us over time?
- What is your sense of—or what are your fears about—how any decision we make to change our relationship to [name of person] will affect [him or her]?

Under *perceived choices*, ask:

- What choices do we have with this issue?
- Is there any compromise open to us regarding the role [name of person] plays in our lives?

Under *needs*, ask your partner:

- What are your needs in regard to how exclusive or inclusive our relationship is?
- What would you identify as your most important, immediate need with regard to the role [name of person] plays in our lives?

- If our relationship to [name of person] were exactly as you'd want it to be, what would this look like?

As you proceed through the interview, write down the main responses your partner gives to each question. Don't correct, refute, or even comment on anything he or she says, unless you're asking for clarification. Conduct yourself in the manner of a neutral journalist trying to get the facts. Remember that hearing and faithfully recording what your partner says doesn't mean you agree with it. Your task now is simply to understand it. (And this is no small thing!)

Doing the exercise alone requires an exceptional degree of emotional honesty and empathy. Really try to step into your partner's skin, profiting from all you've learned about him or her over the years, when you role-play the other side.

If you're working on the exercise with your partner, reverse the process as soon as the interview is complete. The interviewer now becomes the interviewee and answers all the questions he or she just asked.

When you've completed both sides of the interview, whether you're working alone or as a team, you'll have a lot more information about your partner. Chances are that you'll also have some new insights about yourself. You may be able to use this knowledge to usher in a new era of respect and empathy between you. At the very least, you'll have learned to approach your conflicts with more understanding than blame.

Action Plan #2: Wise Mind Meditation

Your conflicts about who to include in your shared life and how much to include them reflect the differences in your needs. This exercise may help you and your partner reconcile your differing desires. If you're absolutely allergic to so-called "New Age" thinking, skip this exercise. Some people find it very helpful; others don't.

Start by writing a one- or two-phrase description of your needs regarding the person who is the source of this conflict in your relationship. If you're working with your partner, have him or her do the same. If either of you has any trouble with this, refer back to what you said about your needs during the Couples Research Interview.

Now sit holding hands. Focus on your breathing. (If you're doing this exercise alone, simply sit comfortably with your hands in your lap.) Notice the sensation of the air flowing in and out of your lungs. Bring your attention to the place where your diaphragm expands when your lungs are full, about two inches above your navel. Breathe deeply; focus on your breath.

After a little while, you may feel a sense of lightness or calm. This is known in Buddhism as "wise mind," a state in which the anger, hurt, or blame you typically feel melts away; a place where it is sometimes possible to see more clearly, more intuitively, than you can at other times. When you reach wise mind, stay there for a few minutes. Keep holding hands, keep noticing your breath.

Now think of the needs each of you wrote down. What solution or compromise would allow each of you some of what you need? Allow wise mind to work on this problem. Don't force it. Just breathe and focus on your diaphragm. Let new ideas slowly emerge. When you're ready, share some of your thoughts with your partner. If you're working alone, write down the thoughts and ideas that came to you. You might want to share these later, in a calm moment with your partner.

10

Trust and Goodwill

Is Long-Term Commitment Possible if These Are Lost to Us?

S andra and Tony were the sort of hybrid couple—professional and blue collar—one finds in big cities all over the United States now. Sandra was a thirty-five-year-old public defender who specialized in the juvenile justice system. She was smart, attractive, and had never been married. She had a fierce dedication to her work that she also applied to her personal life. She told me, when we first spoke on the phone, that she wanted to bring every trick of couple's therapy to bear on her troubled relationship. "But I don't have much hope for it," she added after we'd found a date when I could meet with her and her partner. "I was allowing myself to believe that maybe—just maybe—this was Mr. Right. Just goes to show you how credulous even a woman my age can be."

For the past year, Sandra had been in what she had believed to be a committed relationship with Tony, whom she'd met at a cooking class. Tony was a car mechanic with a master's degree in something called "the history of consciousness"—which turned out to be a bit ironic. But, then again, people say that psychologists are about the most neurotic people you're likely to find. Perhaps many of us are drawn to study what we most long to heal.

I couldn't help liking both these people enormously from the moment they walked into my office. I knew that I'd be quite happy chatting to either of them in any kind of social situation. They were bright and funny and exuded a lot of warmth that shone through the cocky, slightly crusty persona they each seemed to have honed and polished. There was a lot of erotic energy crackling between them and also a lot of anger and resentment zinging around the room.

Tony and Sandra's Commitment Dialogue

Dr. McKay: So, Sandra and Tony—tell me about your situation.

Sandra: As you know, we've been seeing each other for a year. Certain things have happened that have made it apparent to me that our relationship is in big trouble. There has been a series of what I would call clues or indications that Tony has been seeing either another woman or several other women.

Dr. McKay: Tony, I see something in your reaction. What's happening for you?

Tony: Sandra, I think you're really going down the wrong road. You know I see a lot of women every day in my work. Women are coming to me for help with their cars. And maybe that's kind of creating this illusion for you that something's happening that's not happening.

Dr. McKay: So, Tony, this doesn't make any sense to you. You don't know where these ideas and feelings are coming from?

Tony: Paranoia. You know, when you're in a relationship, you've just got to trust each other. There's got to be a certain level, a deep level, at which you just trust.

Dr. McKay: So it's important to you to feel Sandra's trust.

Sandra: Trust? I think the context makes trust a little bit difficult in our situation.

Dr. McKay: What do you mean?

Sandra: Well . . . Tony was in the shower the other morning when I'd stayed overnight at his house. And there was not one, but there were two calls, messages from women that came in on his answering machine. Of course, I don't answer the phone at his house. But I couldn't help hearing these messages; the volume was turned up quite high on his machine. These were both messages from women with whom Tony obviously has a very personal involvement.

Tony: Now, why do you say that? These are just people calling about their cars. They're just clients.

Sandra: Do your clients usually call you "Honey"?

Tony: Those are probably not clients but they're friends. I have a whole bunch of women friends, and I enjoy their company. I don't know why that should be an issue. They call me "Honey" sometimes. And "Tony, you sonuvabitch" sometimes. You know, it depends on how they're feeling on a given day.

Sandra: Tony, there was a Solange and there was Marion. I'm sure you know who these people are?

Tony: They're friends of mine.

Sandra: I haven't met these friends of yours. And I've met quite a few of your friends.

Tony: Well, you don't know all of my friends! I meet people every day. I have several people I've gotten to know in the last few months—

Sandra: Tony, we've been together for a year. It's been an exclusive relationship for a year. I've introduced you to all of my friends, and I thought you'd introduced me to all of your significant friends. But I think you have some very significant friends I don't know about.

Tony: You don't know all of my friends—

Sandra: Evidently I don't.

Tony: And I don't feel the need to introduce you to all of my friends.

Sandra: Was it Solange or was it Marion who left the deodorant in your bathroom?

Tony: What deodorant?

Sandra: The ladies' deodorant. The pink deodorant. I don't imagine it's something you bought for yourself.

Tony: I don't know what you're talking about. But it's probably left over from somebody years ago.

Sandra: It wasn't there last week!

Tony: And what are you doing digging around in my bathroom cabinets anyway?

Sandra: I was looking for a Q-Tip.

Tony: Who knows? Maybe I just moved it when I was cleaning or something. Or maybe it was on sale. I don't know what you're talking about.

Sandra: Shall I show you?

Tony: What?

Sandra: The deodorant: Lady Schick? I don't think this is yours, and I don't think it was something left over from long ago or something you bought by mistake. You're a very orderly man! You're about the most orderly man I've ever met.

Dr. McKay: Tony, let me just step in here for a moment, please. Sandra is presenting what she feels is some evidence that your relationship is not exclusive—that there may be other people that you're involved with. What's happening to you as you listen to this?

Tony: I'm feeling kind of insulted! I feel like I'm in court now and Sandra's trying to trap me into making a confession or something. I feel like I'm in the witness box.

Dr. McKay: From your point of view, there's really no basis for this and you're just kind of getting hit with accusations—

Tony: This is coming from way out in left field!

Sandra: Left field, Tony? Um . . . I have some other things in my purse here. I take birth control pills. And for the last six months of our relationship, that's been the only form of protection we've used. And yet—look what I found when I was looking for Q-Tips in your bathroom!

Tony: Condoms—what do you expect? I mean, I've probably had those for two years. I mean, why should I throw them away? They're expensive. And you've got to be prepared in life. What can I say? I was a Boy Scout. If for some reason things don't work out for us, Sandra, I might need them someday. It's the thrifty housewife in me. It would go against my upbringing to throw them away.

Sandra: I don't think you should throw them away, because I think you should start using them—with me! Because I don't trust you anymore.

Tony: Now I just can't understand why condoms, which I've had for probably years, should be an issue between us.

Sandra: I didn't notice them there before.

Tony: Well, maybe you should have paid more attention.

Sandra: I'm just now starting to pay good attention, Tony. I feel like my eyes are open—they're open for the first time in months. And I'm seeing all kinds of things I would rather not see.

Tony: Well, I'm sorry that you're so suspicious. It probably has something to do with your legal training. This is not the kind of relationship that I want to have. I want to have a relationship where you trust me as much as I trust you. I really trust you, Sandra.

Sandra: I haven't given you any reason to mistrust me!

Dr. McKay: Sandra, you sound very angry right now. This relationship is not turning out the way you'd hoped.

Sandra: No, it is not turning out the way I'd hoped. And, yes, I am angry. I have good reason to be angry, too. I have something else in my purse. Last time I checked, Tony, you were not wearing thongs! And I don't think they're your size *or* your color.

Tony: What are you talking about?

Sandra: These. They are not mine. I found them in your couch—between the cushions when I dropped my pen. They're not yours, are they, baby?

Tony: I don't know what you're—

Sandra: Tony, you are busted. Unless you have an explanation for these, too. Are you a secret cross-dresser? You just have this thing about lingerie? You've been worrying about visible panty lines?

Dr. McKay: Let me interrupt for a minute. Sandra has presented a succession of physical evidence, as well as the telephone messages, that indicate to her that there's a likelihood something is going on—that you're having another relationship or that you have another sexual partner. And I want you to take a moment here, Tony, before you answer me. I want you to think about your answer very carefully. Because the future of this relationship may hinge upon your answer. If it's a relationship you value, then your honesty and authenticity may be all you have right now to prevent you from losing Sandra.

Tony: You know, I feel like I'm damned if I do and damned if I don't. I'm a man. I have a past. And I've had my moments that have been maybe outside the boundaries of what this relationship is supposed to be.

Dr. McKay: Tony, Sandra is bringing evidence that you are having other sexual relationships right now. And I think it's really important, if you want to save this relationship, that you say clearly and honestly what is happening, why it's happening, and what you want in your relationship with Sandra.

Tony: Okay, I'll answer you! I don't know. I don't know. I don't know. Okay? I'm confused.

Dr. McKay: You don't know what's happening.

Tony: I know what's happening! But I don't know what I want. And I don't know why it's happening.

Dr. McKay: Let's start with what is happening. Sandra is finding ladies' deodorant and condoms, even though you and she don't use condoms. She's finding panties. She's listening to calls coming in from other women. She's seeing an awful lot that suggests something is going on in terms of another relationship. Let's start with the facts. Let's start with what is true about you and other people.

Tony: I had a certain lifestyle before I fell in love with Sandra—a lot of opportunities and a lot of involvements. And things—I mean, it's hard for other people to just get used to your life totally changing. It's . . . Okay. Yeah. I had one experience. Maybe two.

Dr. McKay: So you've had maybe two other sexual experiences, and these are going on concomitantly with your relationship with Sandra.

Tony: Yeah.

Dr. McKay: That's a clear, direct statement. What's happening for you, Sandra, right now?

Sandra: I feel so betrayed. First of all, all the lying and bullshitting—I just feel like a fool! Putting a year of my life into this relationship, into trusting Tony. And, also, what am I exposing myself to? We haven't been using condoms. I feel afraid! I mean, who knows what he's been touching, being exposed to? I feel disgusted.

Dr. McKay: So you felt and believed that you had a contract with Tony, a contract and a promise that each of you would be faithful to the other. And learning that Tony has not kept that promise has left you feeling betrayed but also vulnerable, even vulnerable physically.

Sandra: Absolutely. And it sure looks like I can't trust this guy at all. It makes me really question my own judgment.

Dr. McKay: Tony, what's happening to you as you're listening to Sandra talk about feeling betrayed, feeling afraid now that she may be physically endangered because of having unprotected sex with you?

Tony: First of all, I want to reassure her that I used condoms with the other women. So, Sandra, you don't have to worry about that.

Sandra: Oh—like I should really believe you!

Tony: I swear, I didn't expose you to anything. I hate to defend myself, but I was thinking about you in that way. I was.

Dr. McKay: Tony, I want to ask you an important question that will probably determine where we go from here in this therapy process. You made the decision to connect with other people, other women. And I'm wondering, what was going on inside of you that made you feel like that was a good idea?

Tony: It wasn't a conscious decision. I wasn't thinking with my head. It was an opportunity, an invitation—and I just went along with it. It was just the momentum. It wasn't something I sought out—honest to God, it wasn't.

Dr. McKay: When did this start, in terms of your relationship with Sandra? How many months ago?

Tony: Well, it wasn't something that started. I guess it's just some stuff that didn't really end.

Dr. McKay: So these are relationships and people with whom you were connected before Sandra came into your life. And they sort of continued. What do you think would have happened with you and Sandra if you had stopped those relationships way back a year ago— if you had said no to those women and had focused your romantic energy exclusively on Sandra?

Tony: From where I'm sitting now, I can see that that would have been a good idea.

Dr. McKay: I'd like you to imagine that early part of the relationship, where now you've said good-bye to those women. They're not part of your life, and you don't have the energy and the connection and the excitement of looking forward to those liaisons. You're just working on your relationship with Sandra. What happens inside of you without those other women? How does that change your life inside?

Tony: Those words you used—"working on your relationship with Sandra." You make it sound like we're locked away in a room somewhere, working and working. Without anyone else in there. It feels like . . . something's lost.

Dr. McKay: A sense of loss as you imagine letting go of those other people and—

Tony: A loss of excitement. A kind of vacuum.

Sandra: Well isn't that just too sad—the idea of actually having to focus on your relationship with me and give up those other women!

Dr. McKay: I can understand how upsetting this is—and how angry it makes you feel right now. But I think we have an opportunity at this moment, a window, that will allow us to look into what's happening inside of Tony. I think we should take advantage of that. Would you be willing to listen for now and be receptive to whatever it is we're able to learn?

Sandra: I'm all ears.

Dr. McKay: Okay. So, Tony, if you were to give up those relationships; if you were to focus on Sandra without those other women in your life, what would the feeling be? What would it be like inside of you without those other relationships? This is an important question. I want you to think about it a minute. Just imagine your life without those other relationships. What's missing for you? What isn't there?

Tony: I guess it's kind of the mystery—you know, the unknown, the possibility of something unexpected. The lightness, the kind of joyfulness that you get sometimes. The playfulness.

Dr. McKay: Okay. That joyfulness, that playfulness, that mystery—

Sandra: So you're saying, Tony, that . . . what? With me it's all just a grind?

Dr. McKay: This is very hurtful, what you're listening to, Sandra. I can imagine what it must feel like to listen to Tony describe these other relationships and his feelings about them. But at the same time, we have this moment here in which we can learn something very important, and there's a chance it may help. Are you willing to take that chance now? Are you willing to listen for a few moments longer?

Sandra: Yes.

Dr. McKay: Tony, if you really had to face life without that mystery, that excitement, what would that feel like inside? What's the feeling as you imagine life without those experiences?

Tony: I want to start by saying it's got nothing to do with Sandra. Like I said, Sandra is this wonderful woman—

Dr. McKay: I believe you.

Tony: She really is. But, when I think about, you know, total exclusivity, I just feel like . . . this shut-down feeling. Like it's just going to be all work from now on. And there's no escape. It makes me feel kind of panicky.

Dr. McKay: It scares you. How come?

Tony: There's not enough air. It's like a vacuum.

Dr. McKay: A vacuum—you used that word earlier. Would you say that it's a feeling of emptiness? Or do you feel a sense of the walls closing in? What's that feeling?

Tony: It's like the sense of deadness inside me, like an emptiness.

Dr. McKay: So without that excitement, that mystery, that intensity that those other relationships offer, there's this feeling inside of being somehow shut down, muted. Or empty.

Tony: Yeah.

Sandra: Oh my God. He is so self-absorbed, he can't even see the pain he's causing me.

Dr. McKay: You know something, Sandra—the pain you're feeling now is so big and so hurtful, we need to spend time paying attention to it. But right now I'd like to stay focused on trying to learn something about where Tony's betrayal came from. And it may be important—

Sandra: I know where it came from. It came from between his legs!

Dr. McKay: Well, in part it comes from sexual energy. But it also sounds like it comes from a desire to escape or avoid a kind of pain that Tony lives with. So let me go back to Tony for a minute and see if we can just learn a little bit more about that pain, and then I want to hear about your experience as you're listening. So, Tony, that feeling is an emptiness. Tell me more about that.

Tony: I don't know what else to say about it. It's just like needing stimulation. It's like needing other stuff. Needing change. Needing possibility.

Dr. McKay: And if you don't have that—the change, the possibilities, the stimulation—what happens to you? What happens inside of you?

Tony: Like I said, I feel shut down. Not alive. Not vital.

Dr. McKay: Is that something that you've always struggled with in some way?

Tony: Yeah, I guess so.

Dr. McKay: This is something you have feared. You fear being cut off from that vitality.

Tony: I've always liked a lot of stimulation. I guess it's no accident that I'm forty-three years old and I've never been married. And my main mode of transportation is a motorcycle.

Dr. McKay: Let me turn back to you, Sandra. I know that you have a lot of feelings right now. You've been very patient in listening to Tony describe this feeling inside of him that drives him to seek or hold on to other relationships—

Sandra: It's very hard for me to feel sympathetic, listening to him. I feel like it's just an excuse for bad behavior—for moral laziness!

Dr. McKay: So it's hard to imagine that this pain, this emptiness that he experiences, is anything other than a cover for—

Sandra: We all have a lot of pain. Okay, this isn't something Tony has talked about. But it doesn't take away the fact—the essential fact—of his betrayal of my trust. I feel like something that was rather beautiful and whole has been broken, and it's just in too many pieces now. There's no way to glue this thing back together.

Dr. McKay: I hear you. You've been deeply hurt, and your trust has suffered a major blow.

Sandra: I will never be able to trust him again. How could I? I mean, he's not only betrayed me, but then he had the gall to lie to me about it, in front of you. How can I trust this man? How can I hope to have a partnership with this man? I'd be crazy!

Dr. McKay: We're at a point here, where a decision lies in front of us. I'm hearing you say very clearly that the trust is so compromised that you're not sure how it could ever be put back together, or even if it should be put back together. But we also are hearing from Tony, and Tony is saying that this behavior comes from a fear of a feeling of emptiness. A fear that he is going to feel numb, shut off, deadened inside. And it's possible that we could work on that feeling. That we could find ways to help Tony cope with that feeling other than seeking connection to other women. It's possible that we could work on rebuilding your relationship. But I'm wondering, are you at all willing or open to consider that at this moment?

Sandra: I think that if Tony wants to redecorate his interior landscape, he's got his work cut out for him, and I wish him good luck. But, you know what? I don't feel like I want to put another day of energy into this relationship. For me, it's just bankrupt.

Tony: Sandra, don't be too hasty. There's been a lot of good in us. You know it. And we've had a lot of fun. We've had a lot of great times. And I think we could still have great times. Okay, I'm a flawed human being. Nobody's perfect. But I really need you to give me a second chance.

Sandra: You know what, Tony? If I were in my twenties, I would. But I'm not. I'm thirty-five years old, and if I'm going to get into a partnership and have a family, I've got to do it now. I just don't have time to deal with your emptiness or whatever it is, Tony. I wish you good luck—I really do. But I don't have time to work on this relationship any more than I have already.

Dr. McKay: I hear you, Sandra. You're being very clear. For you, at this moment, the most important thing is to rebuild your life and pursue the things you really want, that really matter to you. Tony, I think it's been very brave to both acknowledge infidelity and to open up the part of yourself that drives you to pursue these other relationships—that emptiness, that deadness. And taking the step to acknowledge the fear of those feelings is a real beginning to doing something about them. I suspect that those feelings have been, are now, and may continue to influence your relationships and drive you to do things that undermine the basic commitment and foundation of your primary relationship. The fear of being empty, the fear of feeling deadened, disconnected, unalive is so powerful that it makes you run into the arms of others. Saying out loud, for the first time, what that fear is and how it influences your behavior is a huge step. This relationship is so damaged, it sounds like Sandra is not at this moment ready to consider working on it. But, Tony, if you are ever going to have a successful relationship, with authentic commitment—a relationship that you are not secretly betraying—then these issues need to be confronted and worked on and changed. You will need to face your fear.

Therapist's Overview

It takes time to build trust in any relationship. The way in which trust grows is simple: people keep their promises. They show up when they say they will. They follow through with plans and commitments. They are faithful when they give their word about something.

Trust building is slowed or undermined by two kinds of damaging events.

The first we call *trust punches*—a failure to keep small promises or commitments. Canceling plans at the last minute, bailing out on an offer of help, or reneging on a mutually reached decision might fall into this category. A relationship can sustain a few trust punches, but not many. When they occur frequently, trust starts to erode. If your partner is ambivalent about the relationship *and* delivers regular trust punches, this is a strong signal that you need to let go.

The second kind of damage is outright betrayal. Sexual infidelity, telling sworn secrets, blowing off a major promise, physical assault, and doing any deliberate harm all fall into this category. Here's my rule for dealing with betrayal: if a partner who won't commit also betrays you, end the relationship. Don't wait, don't spend weeks talking about it in therapy, don't consult all your friends. Just go.

You are already struggling in a relationship where something is seriously wrong—your partner is afraid to commit. It's a huge issue that may take all your collective resources to successfully navigate. You can't add in betrayal and have any realistic hope for a good outcome. A serious breach of trust will cripple your efforts to strengthen and deepen your love. The ship is sinking. Get off before it takes you down.

To paraphrase Santayana, those who disregard history are bound to repeat it. This is as true for partners as it is for nations. Lovers who throw frequent trust punches and lovers who betray have little commitment to your well-being. And they are likely to repeat their behavior. People like Tony, in the dialogue you just read, rarely change; and no amount of hoping, wishing, or waiting will make them evolve into who you want them to be. Their overriding concern is their own needs—not yours or the health of the relationship you share.

11

---◆---

Making a Decision

Letting Go Versus Going for It

U p to now we've focused on ways to overcome the four fears underlying most commitment problems. But what about the relationships that will never work, no matter how hard a partner may try? When should you let go? What are the signs that a relationship is fatally flawed?

There are nine key factors to consider in the decision about letting go. Each one of them could be a sufficient reason to say good-bye.

1. Time

How much time have you given to making things work? Commitment questions are a normal part of the early relationship-building process. But by six or twelve months into the relationship, these questions should be resolving themselves. If commitment issues persist beyond one year, it usually suggests

- There's something structurally wrong with the relationship that keeps a partner ambivalent, or
- One of the four underlying fears is at play.

At this point you have a choice—let go or work on it. If you choose to work on it, make sure that you have a firm commitment from your partner to participate in the effort. *And* set a time limit. Agree on a specific period during which—alone or with a therapist—you'll explore the blocks to commitment. If you can't get an agreement from your partner to work on things, or the time limit expires, leave.

A second concern regarding time is the question of how much you have. How loud is your biological clock? Have you put off career or educational decisions while struggling with this relationship? Are you waiting to move somewhere, perhaps to a place where you feel more comfortable or at home? Is there an important goal you've put off?

If time is running out for something you've yearned for and your relationship remains mired in ambivalence, it's probably best to let go. Don't sacrifice your dreams for a relationship so stuck and flawed that it has little chance to succeed.

2. Progress

An important step in evaluating your relationship is to take an honest measure of the progress you've made. Has your partner made significant steps toward commitment—for example, spending more time with you or your family and friends, giving help when you need it, or agreeing to live together? How flexible is your partner in responding to your requests, in making an effort to please you, in trying, at times, to do things your way?

If you don't see a positive trend in some of these key areas—if the basic level of commitment and closeness has remained unchanged and inadequate since the beginning—you should seriously consider whether growth is really possible in this relationship. You need to stop hoping and wishing and take an honest look at your lover's capacity and willingness to meet your needs.

3. How It Feels When You're Together

How you feel is your responsibility. But, without doubt, your partner has a lot of influence on your emotional landscape. Put a check mark by any feeling that occurs at least sometimes when you're together:

_____ *I feel comfortable, safe.*

_____ *I feel loved, cared for.*

_____ *I feel confident in us.*

_____ *I feel close.*

_____ *I feel happy, cheerful.*

_____ *I feel good about myself.*

_____ *I feel optimistic.*

_____ *I feel respected.*

_____ *I feel understood.*

_____ *I feel taken care of.*

_____ *I feel valued.*

_____ *I feel trust.*

_____ *I feel trusted.*

_____ *I feel heard and seen.*

_____ *I feel emotionally satisfied.*

_____ *I feel lonely.*

_____ *I feel anxious, worried.*

_____ *I feel criticized, wrong.*

_____ *I feel shame or embarrassment.*

_____ *I feel sad, disappointed.*

_____ *I feel distrusted.*

_____ *I feel angry.*

_____ *I sense problems ahead.*

_____ *I feel unimportant.*

_____ *I feel distrustful.*

_____ *I feel on my own, unsupported.*

_____ *I feel disrespected.*

_____ *I feel misunderstood.*

_____ *I feel uncomfortable.*

_____ *I feel yearning, emotionally hungry.*

Now look over what you've marked. Do you have more checks in the positive- or negative-feeling column? How often do you feel the positive versus the negative feelings when you're with your partner? Are there any negative feelings that seem so unpleasant or hurtful that they outweigh the positives in this relationship? Has there been a change in recent weeks or months in terms of the balance of positive to negative feelings?

The answers to these questions can help you evaluate whether your commitment issues are worth the struggle. A mostly positive relationship may encourage you to keep working to overcome a partner's ambivalence. But if you're already struggling with significant negatives in a relationship, it may be time to let go.

4. Trust

Do you trust your partner? Does he or she keep promises? Can you count on your partner for help when you need it? Does your partner show up when you are expecting him or her to? If you find that a lover doesn't keep small commitments, you have to assume that they won't keep the big ones, either.

Most partners who are seriously exploring a relationship have a monogamy contract, either explicit or assumed. They commit to being sexually intimate only with each other. There's a good reason for this: it's very hard to build a close, trust-based relationship when there are multiple sexual partners in the picture. The intimacy is defused. Trust and safety are compromised.

There are exceptions to this rule, just as there are exceptions to every rule, but they're rare. Almost every attempt at an open relationship will either eventually blow up over trust and commitment issues or else will evolve finally toward monogamy.

If your relationship doesn't have a clear contract concerning monogamy, ask for one. And should your partner refuse to make that commitment, end the relationship. It doesn't have a future. If your ambivalent partner violates your contract during the first year or two of your evolving relationship, end it. Dealing with betrayal, while also trying to work through commitment struggles, is a setup for failure. The chance of successfully navigating such difficult waters is much too low to justify wasting even more time and effort. (See Chapter 10 for a more detailed discussion of this issue.)

5. Breadth of the Relationship

One of the best predictors of longevity for couples is the breadth of their connection. While differences often attract people, it's what they have in common that holds them together. How many interests do you share? Are your values and life goals compatible? Do you have friends in common; do you like and spend time with each other's families? Do you prefer the same lifestyle? Do you have similar conflict and problem resolution styles?

If a relationship has a narrow-based focus on sex and romance, it may be a lot of fun. But it's like a straw house that can blow down in the first big wind. It's structurally limited.

The breadth of your connection becomes particularly important when dealing with commitment issues. A broad-based relationship, with shared interests and agreement on core lifestyle choices, can often overcome commitment fears. That's because there are more strands of connection, more opportunities that will weave your lives together. But a relationship built primarily on sexual attraction that also has an uncommitted partner is far less likely to endure.

6. Do You Like Yourself When You're Together?

It's a simple question, but one of the most important you can ask. Each relationship acts as a mirror that reflects you a little differently. Do you like who you see in your partner's eyes? Do you like the qualities and traits this relationship brings out in you?

Are there parts of yourself you value that remain unexpressed or unexplored in this relationship? Do you see those parts atrophying if you stay? Or is there scope for these parts of yourself to find expression in other aspects of your life?

If you don't feel good about who you are in this relationship, or the ways in which it limits or defines you, it may not make sense to struggle further with commitment issues. You may want to consider letting go and moving on.

7. Who Does the Work?

Just like plants or children or pets, relationships cannot thrive without being nurtured. A healthy relationship demands that caretaking and problem-solving initiatives be shared by both partners to help sustain and protect your bond.

How much does each of you contribute to this effort? Ledger-keeping can be a bad thing in a relationship if carried too far. But if you're struggling with the question of whether to hang on or let go, it may help to do a little emotional bookkeeping. What's the give-and-take ratio in terms of what each of you contributes and receives? Try out the two simple assessment tools below. They are both highly subjective measures: their usefulness consists in their ability to reveal your feelings about the equitability of your relationship.

Who does the work? The first number represents the percentage of relationship maintenance work that you do; the second number is your partner's percentage. Circle the pair of numbers that reflects your perception of this ratio in your relationship:

10/90   20/80   30/70   40/60   50/50   60/40   70/30   80/20   90/10

Now let's look at your give/take ratio. This refers to the amount of work you each do on tasks that benefit both of you but don't necessarily have to do with relationship maintenance—chores such as doing the cooking and shopping, cleaning the bathrooms, mowing the lawn, maintaining the car. The first number represents the percentage you give, the second is the percentage you get. Circle the pair of numbers that reflects your perception of the give-and-take ratio in your relationship:

10/90   20/80   30/70   40/60   50/50   60/40   70/30   80/20   90/10

If you see yourself as doing most of the giving and most of the work in this relationship, and your partner remains ambivalent, you are probably working too hard for a lost cause.

We would hate to influence anyone to give up on a potentially good relationship without careful thought. But if your relationship is out of balance in terms of the give-and-take, the odds are against its ultimate success. These ratios are not likely to change once they're established. And the long-term consequences of this are feelings of helplessness and depression, because you're doing the heavy lifting in the relationship and getting very little nourishment in return.

If the ratios are more even, and your partner is doing his or her share of the work, there may be hope that you can someday reach commitment even if your partner is ambivalent now.

8. Red Flags

Although love certainly tends to be blind, you should still try to keep your eyes peeled for behavioral red flags. If you see them while also struggling with commitment, the relationship is broken, and you should immediately let go. The primary red flags are:

- Infidelity
- Pathological jealousy—accusing you, following you, checking on you
- Lying about things that matter (as opposed to "white lies")
- A pattern of failing to help you when you're in need
- Physical abuse of any kind
- Emotional abuse—a pattern of denigrating, undermining, or maliciously humiliating you
- A pattern of trying to control you with anger, threats, or emotional or sexual withdrawal
- Disappearing—dropping in and out of your life
- A pattern of treating with contempt things that are truly important to you

- An unacknowledged and/or untreated problem with drinking or substance abuse that is making your partner dysfunctional or undermining your relationship in some other way

Be honest with yourself about red flags. Don't make excuses or hold onto false hopes that such breaches can be survived. They can't, and you need to get out. It doesn't matter how much love, how much attraction, how much emotional investment you have. None of that will make a difference if your partner is exhibiting one or more of these behaviors. When a partner betrays or fails you in this way, it means that he or she doesn't care enough to protect you from harm— or else that he or she is too wounded, too damaged, too weak. Without an extraordinary intervention, none of these things are likely to change. The relationship is destined to fail.

This doesn't mean that you can't or shouldn't feel love and compassion for this person. Some people who can't and shouldn't be partners in a committed love relationship can still be friends. Hang on to as many of the positive parts of your connection to this person as you can, as long as staying connected as a friend doesn't make you feel vulnerable or endangered or impede your ability to get on with your life.

If there is even one red flag on your relationship horizon, don't fool yourself into believing you can fix what's wrong with your partner. You can't. Forget about it.

9. Picture the Future

Close your eyes for a minute. Imagine yourself three, four, five years from now with your partner. Visualize the two of you sitting together, perhaps in a restaurant or on a living room couch. How does the scene look? Study your face—do you seem happy? How about your partner? Are you being honest with yourself as you picture this scene?

When you add up all you know about the relationship and all the questions raised in this chapter, can you picture a future in which the two of you are content, even thriving? Or does the future seem darkened by the issues, fears, and behavior patterns that you struggle with now?

There's a good chance that the future you're seeing now has been brought to you courtesy of your intuition. Pay attention to it. You probably already possess the answers to your most pressing questions about this relationship. Be brave enough to acknowledge them, even if they're not the answers you'd hoped for.

Going for It

If you've carefully evaluated your relationship and you've decided it *is* worth further effort, we have five specific recommendations for how to move forward.

1. **Break the commitment process into discrete steps.** While the "M" word may curl the toes of someone reluctant to commit, suggesting three rather than two nights together per week may feel okay. Or taking the step of exchanging keys. Or leaving clothes at each other's house.

A monogamy contract, which is usually nothing more than a simple verbal promise, should be one of the first steps toward committed partnership. Once you have an agreement, it's reasonable to gradually increase the time you spend together. Along the way, each partner should be integrated into the other's family and circle of friends, as well as merge gradually into each other's living space (unless your agreement specifies other arrangements—which is fine, as long as you both agree on and honor the terms of your contract).

Other intermediate steps involve the commitment to share important feelings, needs, or concerns about each other or the relationship and to share in and participate in events and functions that are important to each of you.

Higher-level steps toward commitment involve living together, commingling resources, making joint purchases, and, sometimes, marriage. But commitment can exist in many forms and with many self-imposed limitations. The trick is for both of you to honor the rules of your particular relationship so that you are each able to thrive.

You don't have to do it all at once. And if you have a commitment-phobic partner, you probably can't. Just make a list of the steps that lie ahead, and concentrate your efforts on that next step.

2. **Set a time frame.** Decide how long you're willing to wait and work toward that next step. Tell your partner explicitly:

- The next step toward commitment you want to take
- That the step is important to you
- That you are willing to work toward that goal for a specific period of time (but, after that, if the step isn't taken, you'll have to reevaluate your own commitment to the relationship)

You can follow the same procedure for each item on your list. If your partner balks at a particular step, negotiate a compromise (see number 4 below) or work on a different step. If your partner refuses to work on *any* step toward commitment, it's a sign that he or she will never make one.

3. **Be clear.** Tell your partner directly that you want a fully committed relationship and that you are investing time and effort toward this goal. Explain that you don't expect it to happen all at once but that you need to see *progress* toward real commitment. Be clear that if the relationship doesn't develop toward commitment, it isn't what you want, and eventually you'll have to let go.

4. **Seek compromise.** If your partner is resisting the next step, ask if there is some middle ground he or she would be willing to consider. Putting too much pressure on your partner is likely to create resistance. If you reduce or even halve the pressure to change, sometimes the person will feel less threatened and more willing to respond to your needs. Make an appointment for a discussion of the issue,

and suggest that each of you show up with at least one compromise solution.

A good compromise is a solution that splits the difference and offers something for each of you. Take the example of Jim and Rhonda. Jim wanted to live together; Rhonda didn't feel ready. They eventually compromised on a plan that had Rhonda de facto living at Jim's house, while she still maintained her old apartment as an office and occasional refuge.

5. **Push through fear.** If you have your own fear of commitment, or you're just plain anxious about the uncertainties of twenty-first-century relationships, two things can happen. The fear can exacerbate your partner's ambivalence, and it can make you reluctant to insist on the next step toward commitment.

Let's be honest. Some fear is good. It makes sense; it warns us of real dangers. So how can you know whether to listen to your fear or face it down? The answer lies in the nine key factors described earlier in this chapter. If you carefully considered each of these criteria, you probably have a pretty good idea about whether your relationship has a future.

A relationship without a future needs someone honest enough to listen to all the emotional signs and warnings—and to gently, clearly, unflinchingly say good-bye. A relationship with a future needs a fearless advocate, someone who will fight to make it work.

"Love is a thing to be learned," D. H. Lawrence said. We learn its power, to build and to desolate. We learn its beauty, the hesitant, whispered words with which we open ourselves for the first time. We learn the way love makes us afraid, makes us run.

If you have a love worth keeping, you must learn something else. To fight for it. Use the skills and techniques in this book. Use your abilities to plan and push. Use all your strength, your caring. Make a commitment.

About the Authors

Matthew McKay, Ph.D.
A writer, poet, and clinical psychologist with twenty-five years' experience helping people change their lives, Matthew McKay is the coauthor of twenty-two psychology self-help books, translated into many different languages. All his books are still in print.

Several of Dr. McKay's books have become standard works of reference for therapists and their patients all over the world. *The Relaxation and Stress Reduction Workbook* has had sales of more than three-quarters of a million copies. *Self-Esteem* has sold half a million copies. Cumulatively, Dr. McKay's books have sold more than two million copies.

In addition to his private practice, Dr. McKay is also clinical director of Haight Ashbury Psychological Services in San Francisco. His poetry, which has appeared in more than fifty literary magazines, was brought together in the 2001 collection, *Lucifer in the Resthome*, as well as in the 2004 volume called *The Yosemite Poems*. A train enthusiast and an experienced media guest, Dr. McKay lives in Berkeley, California, with his wife, Jude McKay, a nurse and author, and their two children, Jordan and Bekah.

Barbara Quick
Barbara Quick is a relationship writer and novelist whose first book, *Northern Edge,* won the Discover prize in 1990. Quick's reviews, essays, and articles have appeared in the *New York Times Book Review, Newsweek, Ms.,* the *Los Angeles Times,* and the *San Francisco Chronicle.* She has written under assignment to *People* magazine and *Cosmopolitan*; her weekly column, "The Gender Dialogues," was featured on MyPrimeTime.com. *Still Friends: Living Happily Ever After . . . Even If Your Marriage Falls Apart* and

Under Her Wing: The Mentors Who Changed Our Lives were both published in 2000. Quick is coauthor of the 2004 bilingual picture book, *Even More/Todavía Más*, with artist Liz McGrath. She is at work on a novel, *Anna Maria Violino, Student of Maestro Vivaldi*.

Quick lives in the San Francisco Bay Area with her twelve-year-old son, Julian. She enjoys learning new languages, gardening, and cooking and is an avid student of Afro-Brazilian and jazz dance.